TACTICAL TIME MANAGEMENT

PRAKASH V. RAO

Tactical Time Management
Copyright © 2023 by Prakash V. Rao

ISBN
978-1-962868-06-8 (Paperback)
978-1-962868-07-5 (eBook)
978-1-962868-05-1 (Hardcover)

TACTICAL TIME MANAGEMENT

BY

PRAKASH V. RAO

Dedicated to Dr. Indira Seshagiri Rao.

Educationist, Mentor, Visionary.

My mother.

ACKNOWLEDGMENTS

To those who light the path I tread, I owe you more than words on this page can express.

To my better half, Dr. Bhavani Rao, who has been my anchor in times of storm and my compass when I've lost my way. Your unwavering support, understanding, and love have made all the difference.

To our dear sons, Ananth and Skanda, you are the very essence of my inspiration. Watching you grow and learning from you both has been one of the most fulfilling experiences of my life. Your youthful energy, relentless questions, and absolute wonder for life propelled me to put pen to paper.

To my dear sister, Akila, whose wisdom, love, and persistent encouragement have been indispensable. Your belief in my capabilities, even when I doubted them, kept me pressing forward.

And to my uncles, aunts, cousins, and the entire family, your unwavering faith, continuous motivation, and the countless conversations about the essence of this book have made it what it is today.

This manuscript is as much yours as it is mine. Without your collective presence, encouragement, and faith, this journey might have been one left untaken. From the depth of my heart, thank you all.

TABLE OF CONTENTS

INTRODUCTION

"Time management."

A phrase echoing in the corners of our bustling lives, urging us to dance with every ticking second. The term reminds us of our daily pursuits, aspirations, and the harmony we try to strike. However, imagine if we could waltz more gracefully through our time? Brian Tracy astutely said, "Every minute you spend in planning saves 10 minutes in execution." Yet, how often do we find our best-laid plans adrift?

Enter: the nuanced interplay of strategic and tactical time management.

1. The difference between strategic and tactical time management

Imagine yourself atop a mountain peak, taking in the vast stretch ahead. From this panoramic view, you see the entire journey, every winding path, every impending challenge. This is **strategic time management** at work. Here, foresight rules. As Stephen Covey would suggest, it's about "beginning with the end in mind." This is where our grand visions reside, our overarching goals set, and the alignment of each step towards those destinations ensured.

However, life seldom offers straight paths.

That's where **tactical time management** shines. Envision yourself traversing a dense forest on that mountain. Surrounded by immediate challenges, you decide swiftly, make quick pivots, and react. In Alan Lakein's philosophy, it's about always pondering: "What is the best use of my time right now?"

Yet, the venerable Earl Nightingale once spotlighted the slight misdirection of the term "time management." He opined, "I don't manage time. No one manages time. I only manage activities in the time that I have." It's an insightful shift in perspective. Time, in its essence, is unyielding. Our dominion lies in what we choose to do within its confines.

2. The natural laws of time management and their implications

Like any graceful dance, our interaction with time too has its natural cadences. These rhythms or "natural laws" of time management guide our every move.

Murphy's Law candidly states, "If something can go wrong, it will." Ah, the unpredictabilities of life, where even the most meticulous plans might falter.

Next, **Parkinson's Law** highlights a unique human tendency, "Work expands so as to fill the time available for its completion." It brings to light our proclivity to stretch tasks or, in contrast, wrap them up just under the wire.

Finally, the **Inevitability of Wait**. David Allen, the architect of the Getting Things Done (GTD) methodology, emphasizes that wait times are unescapable. But with a tactical mindset, these moments can be transformed into golden opportunities.

Hyrum Smith encapsulated the sentiment when he emphasized that managing our time is genuinely about aligning with our values and priorities. These natural laws act as beacons, emphasizing the equilibrium between foresight and adaptability. Echoing Covey's sentiment, it's the art of "putting first things first."

Navigating through this book, we'll delve deeper into this intricate ballet of time management. Drawing upon the profound wisdom of thought leaders like Brian Tracy, David Allen, Stephen Covey, Hyrum Smith, Earl Nightingale, and Alan Lakein, we aim to find our rhythm in the grand dance of life.

However, I am but a humble student of these maestros, and in the words of Isaac Newton, "If I have seen far, it is because I have stood on the shoulders of giants." Their profound insights pave our way.

Let's embark on this enlightening journey, steering with a strategic compass and maneuvering with tactical dexterity, all while dancing gracefully with the precious time we are bestowed with.

PART I

THE BASICS
OF TIME
MANAGEMENT

Effective time management is both an art and a science. In "The Basics of Time Management," we embark on a journey that encapsulates fundamental philosophies, strategies, and tactics essential for mastering the multifaceted domain of time. Each chapter, carefully curated, sheds light on an integral aspect of time management, offering readers a comprehensive foundation.

Chapter 1: Value of Planning:

Delving deep into the philosophical underpinnings and practical implications of planning, this chapter showcases how systematic foresight is pivotal in achieving both daily tasks and monumental life goals.

Chapter 2: Making Lists:

Detailing the quintessential role of lists, this segment unveils the transformative power of organizing thoughts and tasks. Readers are introduced to various list-making techniques, ensuring clarity and purpose.

Chapter 3: Prioritization:

Tackling the ever-present challenge of distinguishing the urgent from the essential, the chapter equips readers with frameworks and tools to prioritize tasks adeptly, optimizing productivity.

Chapter 4: Calendar Management:

Spotlighting the indispensable role of calendars, readers learn the nuances of efficient scheduling, underlined by the essence of adaptability in planning.

Chapter 5: Time Trap:

With insights from Alec Mackenzie, this chapter unravels common time management pitfalls, offering strategies to recognize and surmount them.

Chapter 6: Time Boxing:

Emphasizing the allocation of fixed time periods for tasks, this segment highlights the merits and challenges of the time-boxing approach, illustrating its transformative potential.

Chapter 7: Pomodoro Technique:

Francesco Cirillo's revolutionary method of segmenting work into intervals is elucidated. The chapter sheds light on the benefits and best practices, ensuring readers derive optimal value from the technique.

Chapter 8: The Time Management Process:

As a fitting culmination, this chapter amalgamates the diverse techniques and principles explored, offering readers a cohesive, holistic blueprint for mastering time management.

In summary, "The Basics of Time Management" serves as a guiding beacon, illuminating the path towards time mastery. The carefully curated content ensures that readers are well-equipped with a foundational understanding, poised to translate insights into actionable, effective strategies.

CHAPTER 1

The Importance of Planning

As dawn's golden hue paints the horizon, signaling the commencement of a brand-new day, how often do we pause and ponder about our intended imprints on the vast -+canvas of the next 24 hours? In the relentless pace of modern existence, the ritual of planning—which I like to frame as 'activity control'—sometimes slips into oblivion. Yet, this seemingly unassuming practice holds the key to metamorphose our days from a reactive tumble of events to a proactive work of art. We're about to immerse ourselves into the intricate dance of effective activity control: the paramount art of planning.

Benjamin Franklin's timeless adage, "If you fail to plan, you plan to fail," encapsulates the essence of planning. Without a structured path, even the most fervent aspirations become vulnerable to the whims of distraction and procrastination.

Think about constructing a house. Absent a clear, detailed blueprint, the final edifice might stray far from the dream dwelling you envisioned. Similarly, planning operates as that foundational blueprint for our lives. Without it, our actions, even if diligent, may lack direction and purpose. The question then beckons: Are we merely counting hours, or are we meaningfully stepping towards our envisioned goals?

Stephen Covey brilliantly encapsulated the principle of initiating with a clear endpoint in sight. This wisdom accentuates the soul of planning. It isn't merely about handling tasks in isolation, but ensuring each task aligns in symphony with our grand life vision.

Peter Drucker, a beacon in management thinking, wisely remarked, "The best way to predict the future is to create it." He propagated the idea that the future isn't an arbitrary sequence waiting in the wings; it's sculpted diligently through our present choices. This perspective accentuates the immense power of activity control: by orchestrating our actions today, we chisel our tomorrows. Drucker's words portray an individual not as a passive spectator but as an active architect of their destiny.

Let us peel back the many layers of planning. From the psychological anchoring it bestows to its tangible boosts in efficiency, our voyage promises to be holistic. Interwoven with real-life narratives, scientific studies, and invaluable insights, we'll perceive planning not just as an act but as an art to be mastered.

So, as we embark on this enlightening journey, may this chapter serve as a mirror, reflecting your aspirations, intentions, and goals. With a firm grip on our actions today, we not only foresee but actively shape our future. Let's infuse rhythm, purpose, and a touch of brilliance into our bustling days. Welcome to the transformative realm of planning.

Indeed, planning is not just the mere arrangement of tasks on paper or on a screen; it's a meticulous interplay of understanding, sequencing, and synthesizing various components. As we further navigate through this chapter, we're set to understand the depth and nuances that underlie effective planning, preluding the more specific facets we'll be addressing in the upcoming chapters.

Imagine planning as a tree. Its roots dig deep, symbolizing the core values and long-term visions we hold. The trunk stands for our foundational strategies, and the branches, twigs, and leaves represent the varied tasks, goals, and micro-decisions we make every day. Without the synergy of these components, the tree wouldn't stand tall or flourish. Similarly, in planning, every segment interconnects and impacts the others.

One might argue, why this emphasis on planning when life is so unpredictable? True, life has its own rhythm and surprises, but planning equips us with the agility to pivot, reprioritize, and adapt. By sketching out a roadmap, we're not trying to preordain every twist and turn, but we're better prepared to navigate them. In the consequent chapters, tools like making lists and prioritization will serve as our compass and GPS in this journey.

Efficiency is another layer we'll unearth. Think of efficiency in planning as the art of doing the right things with precision and timeliness, optimizing resources, and minimizing wastage—of time and energy. The intent is not to fill every second of our existence but to make every moment count, ensuring our actions echo with purpose and direction.

And then there's the ultimate synthesis- the Time Management Process. After acquainting ourselves with the individual instruments of planning, we will step back and view the orchestration of these tools in the concert of daily life. This grand finale of the planning section will not be just about the 'what' and 'how,' but the 'when.' It will illuminate how the tapestry of daily, weekly, monthly, and quarterly plans weaves into a cohesive whole.

Drawing a parallel with metacognition, time management does indeed serve as a "meta" activity. While metacognition is a contemplation on the process of thinking itself, time management is that higher-order function where we're not just engaged in activities, but we're actively reflecting upon, controlling, and refining those activities. This bird's-eye view ensures that we don't get lost in the maze of busyness but stay aligned with the overarching goals of our lives.

To encapsulate, the canvas of our life is vast, filled with hues of aspirations, challenges, surprises, and routines. By adopting a meticulous approach to planning, complemented by the tools and strategies we'll delve into, we aim to make every brushstroke on this canvas intentional, meaningful, and harmonious. As we pivot from this foundational exploration into the specifics of planning, let's carry forward the essence of proactive activity control, making each day a deliberate step towards our envisioned masterpiece.

CHAPTER 2

Making Lists

In the ever-evolving dance of time, one tool has consistently proven its merit, providing clarity amidst chaos, order amidst the disordered: the humble list.

Lists are not just random compilations; they're the refined sequences to our rhythmic dance with time. They map out the choreography, allowing us to visualize, prioritize, and realize our ambitions. But what is it about these seemingly straightforward structures that makes them so potent?

The Value of Lists

1. The Power of Visualization

Our minds are vast landscapes, teeming with ideas, aspirations, duties, and more. This expanse, while a testament to human potential, can often lead to feelings of being overwhelmed. Here, lists step in as a savior.

When you pen down tasks, you give form to abstract thoughts. It's akin to setting waypoints on a journey. By jotting down 'Finish report by Thursday' or 'Buy groceries for the week,' you're plotting your course, transforming a nebulous concept into a tangible action. As the renowned Brian Tracy puts it, "Clarity accounts for probably 80% of success and happiness."

2. Prioritization- The Key to Efficiency

Stephen Covey introduced the world to the concept of prioritizing tasks based on urgency and importance. Lists are the perfect vessels to apply this wisdom. Not all listed tasks hold equal significance. By ranking them, you discern the vital few from the trivial many.

Imagine setting up dominoes. If you position them correctly, one nudge can set off a cascading effect. Similarly, tackling the most important task on your list can create momentum for others.

3. The Psychological Boost of Achievement

Remember the thrill of coloring inside the lines as a child? Lists offer a similar gratification to our adult selves. Every time you cross off a task, it's a small nod to your accomplishments. Alan Lakein aptly said, "Time = Life; therefore, waste your time and waste your life, or master your time and master your life." And each stroke of your pen, marking a task as done, reinforces your mastery over time.

This might seem minor, but in the grand scheme, these micro-moments of achievement compound, leading to increased motivation and a sense of purpose.

4. A Remedy for Forgetfulness

Amidst life's hustle and bustle, it's human to forget. Be it the promise to call a friend, pick up laundry, or finalize a project blueprint; our brains can sometimes let these slip. Lists act as external memory aids. By laying tasks out in a tangible form, they serve as consistent reminders, ensuring that no commitment, big or small, falls through the cracks.

5. Flexibility and Adaptation

Lists are not rigid entities; they're fluid. As David Allen emphasizes with his GTD method, it's essential to review and adjust. Sometimes, priorities shift. New urgencies emerge. A well-maintained list is adaptable. It allows for real-time adjustments, ensuring you remain aligned with your objectives, even amidst changes.

6. The Peace of an Externalized Mind

Hyrum Smith often spoke about aligning actions with core values. By offloading tasks from your mind to a list, you free mental bandwidth. This liberated space allows for introspection, aligning daily actions with deeper values. It's not just about doing more; it's about doing more of what truly matters.

Crafting Effective Lists

So, how does one go about crafting these compasses of clarity?

1. **Begin With a Brain Dump**: Before organizing, lay out every task, every commitment, every idea. This unfiltered flow ensures nothing is missed.

2. **Categorize**: Group tasks. Personal. Professional. Immediate. Long-term. This segmentation offers clearer focus.

3. **Prioritize**: Not all tasks are born equal. Determine their significance. Use techniques like the Eisenhower Box or the ABCD prioritization method to rank them.

4. **Break Down Large Tasks**: A task like 'Plan the annual conference' can be daunting. But 'Book the venue for the annual conference' is actionable. Breaking tasks into sub-tasks makes them more approachable.

5. **Review and Adjust**: As days unfold, revisit your list. Adjust for new developments. Remember, the list is a living entity, reflecting your evolving dance with time.

In conclusion, lists are more than mere tools; they're companions on our journey through time. They lend clarity, offer direction, and celebrate our achievements. They remind us, as Earl Nightingale aptly put it, to manage our activities in the time we have, ensuring that our dance with time is as graceful as it is purposeful. As we journey ahead, may our lists be the compasses that guide, the milestones that motivate, and the records of our relentless pursuit towards mastering our time and, by extension, our lives.

CHAPTER 3

Prioritization

Life often feels like an overflowing basket of tasks, desires, responsibilities, and dreams. The sheer volume can be overwhelming. However, not all these tasks carry the same weight. Prioritization is the compass that guides us through this jungle of demands. Without it, we find ourselves lost, constantly reacting to what appears before us rather than proactively shaping our path.

Imagine an orchestra without a conductor. Every instrument is critical, but without someone to prioritize and guide the sequence of play, the resulting sound is chaos, not music. Our tasks and responsibilities are those instruments, and prioritization is the conductor.

In the animated world of "The Incredibles," the villain, Syndrome, has a memorable line: "When everyone is super, no one is." This sentiment can be aptly applied to our tasks and commitments. When every task is seen as paramount, the reality is that none of them truly are. The urgency of one task diminishes the importance of another. The key is to discern which tasks genuinely merit our immediate attention and which ones can wait.

This idea is reminiscent of George Orwell's "Animal Farm," where it's humorously stated, "All animals are equal, but some animals are more equal than others." In the realm of our tasks, this translates to the fact that while all our tasks have value, some inherently demand more urgency or hold more significance in the broader tapestry of our goals.

The Essence of Prioritization

Prioritization is not about labeling tasks as 'important' or 'unimportant' in a vacuum. It's about understanding the relative importance of tasks in alignment with our personal and professional goals. It's the process of determining which tasks will bring us closer to our goals, which ones will maintain our current position, and which ones might be distractions or even move us further from our objectives.

The Danger of No Prioritization

Without prioritization, we fall into the trap of the 'tyranny of the urgent.' This means we spend our days in a reactive mode, addressing tasks based on their perceived urgency rather than their true importance. Just because something is urgent doesn't mean it's significant. And many truly vital tasks never scream for attention but silently wait. Over time, neglecting these can have profound consequences.

The Benefits of Prioritization

1. **Clear Direction:** With a clear sense of priority, we have a roadmap. We know where to start and where we're headed.

2. **Optimal Use of Time:** By knowing which tasks to tackle first, we ensure that our best energy is spent on the most significant tasks.

3. **Reduced Stress:** When tasks are prioritized, the overwhelm of too many tasks diminishes. We can focus on one thing at a time, knowing that we're addressing tasks in the right order.

4. **Achievement of Goals:** Tasks aligned with our goals get completed faster, ensuring steady progress towards what we desire.

Methods for Prioritization

There are various tools and methods to help prioritize tasks effectively. Some are complex, while others are straightforward. In the following sections, we will delve deep into several of these, exploring their nuances and applications.

Prioritization is both an art and a science. It requires introspection, understanding our goals, and sometimes even the courage to say 'no' or 'not now.' It's a skill that, when honed, can revolutionize our productivity and satisfaction levels. As we proceed on this journey of time management, always remember: not all tasks are created equal. It's up to us to discern, decide, and direct our energies where they matter most.

Value Pyramid

The pursuit of a meaningful life often leads us to confront a seminal question: What do we truly value? This quest for clarity finds resonance in Hyrum Smith's Value Pyramid, a poignant technique that stands as a testament to aligning our tasks with our core values.

Smith's Value Pyramid is built on a foundational belief: our most authentic selves emerge when our daily actions reflect our deeply-held values. But how does one navigate the intricate dance of desires, obligations, and societal expectations to unearth these values?

1.   Beliefs: Our Inner Truths

At the foundation of the pyramid lie our Beliefs. Just as the foundation of a house determines its strength and stability, our beliefs set the groundwork for our lives. They are the deep-seated convictions we hold, often shaped by our upbringing, personal experiences, or the lessons we've learned throughout our journey. For instance, a person raised in a family that emphasized the significance of community and togetherness might have a firm belief in the importance of strong relationships. Similarly, someone who has faced hardships and come out stronger might possess an unwavering belief in resilience and the ability to overcome challenges.

2.   Values: Our Guiding Principles

Building upon our foundation of beliefs, we have our Values, the walls that give structure to our life's house. These are the principles that direct our daily decisions, molded by the beliefs we hold. Drawing from our previous example, if someone believes deeply in the power of community and relationships, they might value trust, loyalty, and collaboration. On the other hand, an individual who believes in resilience might value perseverance, adaptability, and optimism. When faced with a challenge, the latter might be more inclined to view it as a temporary setback, drawing strength from their past experiences and their value of optimism.

3. Actions: Walking the Talk

The roof of our house represents our Actions, the tangible behaviors and choices we exhibit daily. These actions, ideally, are in harmony with our values and beliefs. Let's delve into our examples. The person who values trust and collaboration, believing in the strength of relationships, might be the first to offer help to a neighbor or may prioritize spending quality time with family over individual pursuits. Conversely, someone valuing perseverance, rooted in their belief in resilience, might persist in the face of adversity, whether it's pushing through a tough project at work or maintaining a positive attitude during trying times.

When all three layers align— when our daily actions reflect our values, which in turn are grounded in our core beliefs— we achieve a state of congruence and deep satisfaction. We're not merely drifting through life but navigating it with purpose and clarity, echoing the wisdom of the Value Pyramid.

So, why is this pyramid important? It's simple. In today's busy world, we're constantly juggling tasks. But not every task is equal. Some tasks make us feel good and fulfilled because they align with our deeper values. Others, not so much. As the saying in 'The Incredibles' goes, "When everyone is super, no one is." Similarly, if we treat every task as equally important, we might miss out on what truly matters.

Hyrum Smith's Value Pyramid reminds us of this. It's a call to take a step back, to reflect, and to make sure our actions match what we truly value. It's about making sure our daily to-dos aren't just about getting things done, but about getting the *right* things done.

Remember, life is short. By using tools like the Value Pyramid, we can make sure we're spending our time on what truly matters, leading to a more fulfilling and purposeful life.

Big Rock Theory

In the vast tapestry of life's obligations, discerning what truly merits our time and energy can be a perplexing endeavor. The Big Rock Theory, an evocative metaphor, unveils the nuances of prioritization in a tangible manner.

Visualize this scenario: A seasoned professor enters his classroom, armed with a series of items: a large clear beaker, three bags filled respectively with big rocks, pebbles, and sand, and lastly, a pitcher of water. With a challenging gleam in his eyes, he presents his students with a riddle- can all these elements harmoniously coexist within the confines of the beaker?

Initially, he pours the sand, then the pebbles, and attempts to nestle the big rocks on top. The results are predictably chaotic, with no room for the big rocks. However, on his second attempt, the professor strategically places the big rocks first, allows the pebbles to find their spaces in between, and then lets the sand filter through the gaps. Just when the class thinks the beaker is full, the professor pours in the water, which seamlessly occupies the minute spaces between the sand granules. The room resonates with a mix of admiration and understanding.

The beaker stands as a representation of our daily 24 hours.

The big rocks are emblematic of our cardinal goals and priorities, the non-negotiable aspects of our lives that lend it profound meaning.

The pebbles, meanwhile, symbolize tasks of secondary importance. They matter but shouldn't overshadow our paramount pursuits.

The sand signifies the smaller, often inconsequential distractions that pepper our day.

But what about the water? The water embodies the unforeseen moments, the unexpected tasks, and the adaptability we must have in our schedules. Even when we believe our day is packed to the brim, life often throws us curveballs, and we must have the flexibility to adapt and accommodate.

The Big Rock Theory isn't just about the significance of prioritization; it's about the essence of adaptability and resilience. Even when our schedules seem jam-packed, there's always room for adjustments, much like how water finds its way amidst the seemingly 'full' beaker. The lesson is lucid: always start with what's most important. Once you've accommodated your primary goals, the secondary tasks, minor distractions, and even unforeseen challenges can be maneuvered around them.

In the grand orchestration of life, this metaphor acts as a compass, steering us back to what's truly essential. It's a poignant reminder to not let the 'urgent' overshadow the 'important.' And even in the densest of schedules, there's always a way to make things work, just as water finds its space. So, as we navigate the myriad challenges of life, let's ensure our 'big rocks' are never sidelined. After all, prioritization coupled with adaptability paves the path to fulfillment.

The A-1 Technique

In the vast panorama of our lives, teeming with ambitions, responsibilities, and desires, there emerges a need for a guiding star. This luminescent beacon is the act of prioritization. Prioritization is more than mere organization; it's the essence of ensuring our energies and efforts are funneled towards actions that resonate with our true self and our envisioned future.

The heart of prioritization rests upon a simple yet profound understanding: It's not always about doing things in the best manner, but rather, it's about choosing the best things to do. In a world inundated with distractions, obligations, and ceaseless demands, making conscious choices becomes our anchor. Each decision, when rooted in thoughtful prioritization, becomes a step towards a purposeful life, where every moment is spent in alignment with our core beliefs and long-term goals.

One might ask, how do we navigate this complex web of tasks and decide which ones are truly deserving of our attention and energy? Here, the wisdom of Alan Lakein's A-1 technique shines brightly. Lakein, recognizing the intricate dance of daily responsibilities, proposed a simple yet effective categorization. He imagined tasks as a spectrum of significance.

A-Tasks: The Pivotal Priorities

A-tasks are your top-tier tasks, the ones that carry a pressing sense of urgency and importance. They're the game-changers, the tasks that hold significant consequences if not addressed promptly.

Example: Imagine you're a project manager. Your A-task might be finalizing and submitting a project proposal due tomorrow that could land your company a major client. Another A-task could be addressing a sudden issue that has halted a project's progress. It's these A-tasks that often sit heavily on our minds, urging immediate action.

Within this A category, the A-1 task is the crème de la crème. It's the task that, when tackled, can significantly propel other tasks forward or even render some of them unnecessary.

Example: In the realm of personal finance, an A-1 task might be paying off a high-interest debt, which once tackled, frees up funds for other endeavors and alleviates financial stress.

B-Tasks: The Significant Secondaries

B-tasks, while important, don't carry the immediate urgency that A-tasks do. They're essential but don't have dire consequences if left for a day or two.

Example: Using the project manager lens again, a B-task might be brainstorming ideas for a future project or reviewing the feedback on a completed project. While these tasks are vital for continuous growth and improvement, they might not need immediate resolution within the day.

C-Tasks: The Comfortable Completions

C-tasks are activities that are nice to tackle but aren't pressing. They're tasks that, if left undone, won't drastically disrupt our workflow or progress. They can often be addressed in the gaps between the more pressing tasks or even delegated.

Example: For many, a C-task might be reorganizing their workstation. While a tidy workspace can boost productivity, it's not imperative to complete the task immediately for most roles.

In essence, by framing tasks as A, B, or C, Lakein gifts us with the lens of clarity. The everyday hustle often blurs the lines between what's truly urgent and what just appears to be. By categorizing tasks, we gain clarity. It's like setting the GPS for our day—knowing what destinations (tasks) to prioritize ensures a smoother, more purposeful journey.

Alan Lakein is immortalized by a simple yet profound question he tells us to ask ourselves: **What is the best use of my time right now?**

The answer, clearly, is **A-1!**

Alan Lakein's technique isn't merely a systematic approach; it's a way of life. It's about moving from a reactive stance, where we're perpetually on the back foot, to a proactive one. By zeroing in on our A-1 tasks, we channel our peak energy and focus where they make the most significant impact. Instead of merely responding to life's demands, we take charge, steering our course deliberately.

But beyond the categorizations and the tasks, lies the true essence of prioritization. It's a pledge to oneself. A commitment that we won't scatter our energies aimlessly, but instead, direct them with intent. By consciously selecting and attending to what genuinely holds value, we sculpt a life enriched with purpose and profound satisfaction.

In sum, as we sail the vast sea of life with countless destinations calling out to us, prioritization is our map. It reminds us to chart our course not by every beckoning shore, but by the stars– our deepest values and dreams– guiding us to a journey not just of accomplishment but of true fulfillment.

Eisenhower Box/Covey Quadrants

In the vast landscape of our daily tasks, a guiding compass is often required to navigate through the myriad commitments, responsibilities, and desires that call for our attention. This compass, offering clarity amidst chaos, is provided by the Eisenhower Box, further refined and popularized by Stephen Covey as the Covey Quadrants. Rooted in a systematic approach to task categorization, this tool has emerged as a cornerstone in the realm of effective time management.

The Eisenhower Box, named after the 34th U.S. President Dwight D. Eisenhower, hinges on a principle that while all tasks demand our attention, not all deserve it in equal measure. By classifying tasks based on two criteria- urgency and importance- this methodology provides a clear matrix to make informed decisions on task prioritization.

Let's delve into the specifics of this matrix:

Quadrant I: Urgent and Important - The "Crisis" Quadrant

Life is replete with unexpected urgencies that call for our immediate intervention. Quadrant I typifies these situations. Beyond just the workplace system malfunction or the imminent threat of a flooded home due to plumbing issues, think of deadlines that sneak up on you, or sudden health emergencies that necessitate immediate care. A child falls and needs to be rushed to the hospital or a crucial client calls with a complaint that threatens your business relationship. These tasks, unexpected and pressing, often arise from unanticipated events or, occasionally, from lapses in foresight or proactive measures. Managing Quadrant I effectively requires swift decision-making, resilience, and often a degree of improvisation. Navigating this quadrant, while inevitable at times, also teaches us the importance of proactive planning to minimize such emergencies.

Quadrant II: Not Urgent but Important - The Growth Quadrant

Quadrant II is the realm of growth, self-improvement, and strategic advancement. Here, we find activities such as setting long-term goals, investing in self-improvement courses, cultivating relationships, or perhaps reading a book that offers personal or professional insights. An entrepreneur might identify a future market trend and strategize accordingly. A parent might spend quality time with their child, nurturing the bond. These tasks, though lacking immediate urgency, are pivotal in shaping our future. Covey emphasizes that this quadrant is crucial for true effectiveness. Investing time here means not only personal and professional growth but also preemptively addressing issues that could otherwise escalate to Quadrant I.

Quadrant III: Urgent but Not Important - The Deception Quadrant

Tasks in this quadrant often come masked as urgent, loudly demanding our attention. Answering every phone call immediately, consistently attending meetings without clear agendas, or constantly reacting to emails can often be classified here. For example, you might be engrossed in a crucial task when a colleague barges in, seeking input on a matter that doesn't pertain to your core objectives. While these tasks cry out to be addressed immediately, they often don't contribute significantly to our broader vision. Discerning management of Quadrant III ensures that while we address external urgencies, they don't sidetrack us from our primary pursuits.

Quadrant IV: Neither Urgent nor Important - The Distraction Quadrant

We've all had moments of seeking refuge in the mindless meanderings of the internet, perhaps browsing videos or getting engrossed in unproductive office banter. While such activities can offer short-term relaxation, excessive indulgence risks turning them into significant time drains. Quadrant IV is where we place tasks that neither align with our core goals nor demand immediacy.

Occasional engagement might serve as a breather, but constant immersion can lead to dissatisfaction, inertia, and a feeling of "where did my day go?" Recognizing and consciously limiting our time in this quadrant helps maintain a balance between relaxation and productivity.

The genius of the Eisenhower Box/Covey Quadrants lies in its simplicity. By visualizing our tasks within this framework, we gain the clarity to act with purpose. The quadrants become our guiding light, illuminating which tasks to tackle immediately, which ones to schedule, which to delegate, and which to discard altogether.

Stephen Covey's endorsement of Quadrant II tasks is particularly significant. In his seminal work, he urged individuals to be proactive, emphasizing that true effectiveness arises when our actions are rooted in our principles and aligned with our end goals. By focusing on Quadrant II, we transition from a reactive stance, where we are constantly responding to external stimuli, to a proactive posture, where we are creating our desired future.

On the other hand, we cannot escape Quadrant I. Crises are inevitable. There will be situations where we must handle urgent and important tasks. We cannot ignore fires or other life-or-death calamities. My advice for such necessary forays into Quadrant I is: do the task twice. In a reactive mode, we cannot think things through. Therefore, do enough to take care of the situation for the nonce and come back to take care of the situation for all time.

In the vast tapestry of time management methodologies, the Eisenhower Box/Covey Quadrants stands out, serving as a beacon guiding us towards conscious, purpose-driven actions.

David Allen's GTD and the 4 D's

In our quest for effective time management, David Allen's "Getting Things Done" (GTD) emerges as a holistic methodology, designed to provide clarity, focus, and a systematic approach to our ever-expanding list of tasks. Allen's GTD, when married to the simplicity of the 4 D's- Do, Defer, Delegate, and Delete- becomes an efficient machine, driving productivity with precision and purpose.

GTD: The Philosophy

David Allen's groundbreaking "Getting Things Done" (GTD) methodology offers a transformative approach to task management and productivity. At its heart, GTD rests on a fundamental principle: our minds, as powerful and vast as they are, aren't built to juggle and retain the minutiae of every task, commitment, or idea. Instead, they thrive when they are liberated to do what they do best: think, create, innovate, and strategize. Holding onto every thought or to-do item clutters our mental workspace, impeding our ability to think freely and strategically.

To combat this, Allen's GTD champions the concept of transferring these tasks and ideas from the mind to an external system. This could be anything from a sophisticated digital tool to a humble notebook. The act of recording tasks externally offers a twofold advantage. Firstly, it ensures that nothing falls through the cracks. Each commitment, no matter how minuscule, is accounted for. Secondly, and perhaps more importantly, it lightens the cognitive burden, allowing the brain to breathe and operate optimally.

To further streamline the process, GTD breaks tasks down into two central categories: Projects and Next Actions. Here, 'Projects' don't just pertain to mammoth tasks but represent any endeavor requiring more than one action. This could be anything from organizing a birthday party to launching a new product. By identifying and categorizing such multi-step tasks as projects, we get a clearer, birds-eye view of the journey ahead.

However, while having an overview is essential, progress is made on the ground, one step at a time. This is where 'Next Actions' come into play. Instead of getting overwhelmed by the entirety of a project, GTD teaches us to focus on the immediate, tangible next step– the very next action we can undertake to move the project forward. For instance, if the project is "Organize a birthday party," the next action might be "Call the bakery for cake options." By focusing on actionable steps, GTD demystifies and simplifies complex projects, making them more approachable and achievable.

In essence, David Allen's GTD is more than just a productivity system; it's a philosophy of work and life. By offloading tasks to an external system and breaking them into actionable chunks, we're not just optimizing our to-do lists but are creating a conducive mental environment, one where creativity, clarity, and strategic thought flourish.

The 4 D's: A Simplified Approach

The essence of the 4 D's lies in providing immediate decisions for incoming tasks, ensuring that tasks don't stagnate, leading to decision fatigue.

- **Do (Quadrant I):** In the world of time management and prioritization, the tasks that fall under Quadrant I are the "front-burner" tasks. Imagine you're a chef, and suddenly one of your stoves catches fire– you don't ponder or deliberate; you tackle that fire instantly. Similarly, if a task is both urgent and important, it's like that stove fire, demanding your immediate attention. For instance, if you're in a professional setting and a client needs an urgent update before an imminent meeting, this becomes a Quadrant I task. The repercussions of not addressing it promptly—losing the client's trust, hampering business relationships, or missing out on opportunities—can be significant. In personal contexts, it could be something like attending to a sick family member. The nature of these tasks is such that they resonate with immediate goals or have impending consequences. Addressing them promptly ensures that the situation is contained, managed, and resolved before it escalates.

- **Defer (Quadrant II, do after Quadrant I tasks are addressed):** Quadrant II tasks are akin to the ingredients you've prepared but haven't started cooking yet in our chef scenario. They're important components of the meal, but they can wait until the stove fire (Quadrant I) is handled. These tasks, while valuable, lack the immediate urgency that characterizes Quadrant I. They are the building blocks for future endeavors, be it planning a new business strategy or setting personal growth milestones, like signing up for a course. For a student, studying for an exam two weeks away can fall into this quadrant. However, the essence lies in understanding that to 'defer' doesn't mean to indefinitely 'postpone' or 'ignore'. It's about strategically scheduling them for a later time, ensuring that once the immediate crises (Quadrant I tasks) are handled, these are the next in line. Regularly diving into Quadrant II ensures a steady path towards achieving long-term objectives and aspirations.

- **Delegate (Quadrant III):** Imagine our chef having many dishes to prepare simultaneously. While the main dish (Quadrant I) requires his expertise, side dishes (Quadrant III) might be handed over to his assistants. In life, some tasks need immediate attention but may not necessarily align with your core objectives. For a manager, this might mean having to prepare a presentation on a topic they aren't familiar with. Instead of spending hours researching and creating it from scratch, they might delegate the initial research to a team member, ensuring efficient time usage. Delegation isn't about shirking responsibility, but rather about optimizing resources. By recognizing tasks that others can execute effectively, one frees up personal bandwidth for more critical activities, thereby ensuring optimal time utilization. Proper delegation leverages the collective strength of a team, allowing for streamlined operations and effective time management. When delegating:

1. **Delegate to Trusted Individuals:** Delegation is an essential skill in both professional and personal arenas, but its success hinges on the choice of the delegate. Handing over tasks or responsibilities to someone else isn't just about lightening one's own load—it's about ensuring that the task finds its way to the best-suited hands. This necessitates trust. By choosing a reliable individual, one ensures that the task is in capable hands, mitigating the need for constant check-ins or revisions. In a work setting, this might mean delegating a project to a seasoned team member with a track record of delivering results. In a personal context, it could translate to entrusting a key responsibility to a family member who has demonstrated competence in that area. When tasks are handed over to trustworthy individuals, it fosters an environment of mutual respect, accountability, and efficiency.

2. **Avoid Micromanagement:** Delegation comes with an implicit pact of trust. When you delegate a task, it's essential to allow the individual the autonomy to execute it in their way. Micromanaging, or excessively overseeing every tiny detail, not only

strains the rapport between the delegator and the delegate but also impedes the very essence of delegation. The person entrusted with the task can feel stifled, undervalued, and under constant scrutiny, hampering their creativity and productivity. Moreover, if a leader is consumed with micromanaging, they miss out on focusing on their core responsibilities. Effective delegation involves setting clear expectations, providing necessary resources, and then stepping back to let the individual deliver.

3. **Match Weaknesses with Strengths:** Self-awareness is a critical asset. Recognizing areas where one might not be the strongest allows for the strategic delegation of such tasks to those who possess strengths in those areas. This symbiotic approach ensures tasks are handled with expertise and dexterity. For instance, if a business leader struggles with the nuances of digital marketing but has an employee who thrives in this domain, delegating related tasks to this individual is a win-win. The task is executed with proficiency, and the leader can focus on areas where they shine. This

method of delegation not only leads to optimal results but also fosters a collaborative environment where individuals' unique strengths are recognized and leveraged for the collective good.

- **Delete (Quadrant IV):** Picture a gardener meticulously tending to a garden. Amidst the vibrant flowers and essential plants, there often sprout weeds. While these weeds might seem inconsequential, if left unchecked, they can overrun the garden, stifling the growth of the desired plants. In the realm of time management, Quadrant IV tasks are akin to these weeds. They are the tasks that, upon reflection, neither push us closer to our immediate objectives nor align with our long-term goals. They are neither urgent nor particularly meaningful.

Take, for instance, the hours one might spend aimlessly scrolling through a social media feed, getting engrossed in a video game with no real end, or indulging in office gossip. While occasional breaks and diversions can be refreshing, spending excessive amounts of time on such Quadrant IV activities can be counterproductive. It's not just about the hours lost; it's also about the opportunity cost—the essential tasks or rejuvenating activities you could have pursued in that time.

Another example could be attending meetings that have no direct relevance to your work or goals. While the intent might be to stay informed or be present, if these meetings don't offer actionable insights or value, they might just be eating into your productive hours.

In a world where time is a finite resource, the "Delete" strategy serves as a filter, ensuring that we don't clog our schedules with non-essential tasks. Regularly reviewing tasks and pruning out the Quadrant IV activities can lead to a more focused, purpose-driven routine. It's about recognizing that just because something can be done doesn't mean it should be done, especially if it detracts from tasks that genuinely matter. By actively choosing to eliminate or reduce time spent on these tasks, we reclaim valuable moments and redirect our energies towards more impactful endeavors.

Interlinking The 4 D's with Covey Quadrants

The beauty of combining Allen's GTD and the 4 D's with Covey's Quadrants lies in the harmonization of two powerful systems.

While the quadrants offer a clear visualization of where tasks stand in terms of urgency and importance, the 4 D's provide actionable steps. The mapping is intuitive:

- Tasks screaming for immediate attention (Quadrant I) are tackled first (Do).
- Important but not pressing tasks (Quadrant II) are deferred but not overlooked.
- Urgent but less important tasks (Quadrant III) are delegated, ensuring they're addressed without draining your personal resources.
- Tasks that don't contribute significantly (Quadrant IV) are ruthlessly deleted.

In conclusion, the amalgamation of David Allen's GTD, the 4 D's, and Covey's Quadrants offers a holistic, actionable system for time management. By categorizing, deciding, and acting based on these combined principles, one is equipped to navigate the intricate dance of daily responsibilities with grace, clarity, and efficiency.

Other Techniques in Prioritization

The 2-Minute Rule

In the bustling rhythm of our day-to-day lives, we often encounter tasks that, while quick to execute, are frequently postponed. David Allen, with his GTD approach, brings forth a simple yet impactful solution to this common challenge: the 2-Minute Rule. The premise of this rule is as straightforward as its name suggests— if a task takes less than two minutes to complete, it should be done immediately.

For instance, let's consider a scenario where amidst a busy workday, you receive an email that requires just a brief reply. Instead of flagging it for later, the 2-Minute Rule encourages you to respond to it right away. Or perhaps, after a meeting, you think of a vital point to discuss in the next session. Instead of relegating it to the backburner, you quickly jot it down, ensuring the idea isn't lost. Similarly, after a meal, instead of leaving the dishes in the sink, if it's a matter of a couple of minutes, you wash them immediately, preventing a build-up.

The beauty of this rule lies in its dual benefits. Firstly, it efficiently prevents the accumulation of a multitude of small tasks, which, when bundled together, can become overwhelming. Secondly, every time you apply this rule and accomplish the task at hand, it provides a quick win, boosting your morale and setting a positive tone for the day. This act of promptness not only declutters our physical workspace but also our mental space, fostering a proactive mindset and a tangible sense of achievement.

The Pareto Principle

In the late 19th century, Vilfredo Pareto, an astute Italian economist, made a keen observation: a mere 20% of Italy's populace owned a whopping 80% of its land. While this insight was initially a comment on the skewed wealth distribution, it laid the groundwork for a principle that would find its resonance across various spheres: The Pareto Principle, commonly termed the 80/20 rule. The essence of this principle is the idea that a significant majority of effects (around 80%) can often be traced back to a small set of causes (roughly 20%).

Translating this to the realm of time management and productivity offers a profound perspective. It compels us to evaluate our tasks and pinpoint that crucial 20% which holds the potential to yield 80% of our desired results. Take the world of business as an example. Imagine a company with a diverse clientele. Upon close examination, they might discover that just 20% of their clients are responsible for 80% of their total revenue. In another scenario, a student might find that concentrating on 20% of the study material garners 80% of the exam's marks.

The underlying message of the Pareto Principle is clear: not all tasks are created equal. By identifying and channeling our efforts towards that pivotal 20%, we optimize our input to achieve maximum output. This approach not only streamlines our efforts but also enhances the quality of our results. The Pareto Principle, thus, acts as a beacon, guiding us to invest our time and resources wisely, enabling informed decision-making, and fostering efficient prioritization.

The ABCDE Method

Juggling the myriad tasks that each day brings can be a daunting challenge. To ensure that we aren't lost in the woods of responsibilities, we need a reliable compass, and the ABCDE method serves as that navigational tool. It stands as a testament to the systematic classification of tasks, aiding in prioritizing them based on their weight and urgency.

- **A-Tasks**: Picture this— you have a project presentation at work tomorrow, which could potentially influence your performance review. Such a task would be categorized as an A-task. It's an absolute must-do and is non-negotiable. Deferring or neglecting it could result in severe consequences, be it missing out on a business deal, suffering academic setbacks, or even straining a significant relationship.

- **B-Tasks**: Now imagine you promised to attend a colleague's farewell two days from now. Missing it might not have monumental implications, but it could slightly dent your rapport with your team. B-tasks are essential, but they allow for a bit of flexibility in their execution, compared to A-tasks.

- **C-Tasks**: Think of activities like reading that book you recently bought or trying out a new recipe. These tasks enhance the quality of life, but their postponement won't throw your life off balance. They're the tasks you'd like to indulge in, but there's no urgency pressing upon them.

- **D-Tasks**: Suppose you have a report to file, but you're swamped with A-tasks. You could delegate it to an intern or a subordinate. D-tasks are those responsibilities that, while necessary, don't necessarily require your personal touch. They can be handed over to others, ensuring they're completed while allowing you to focus on tasks that demand your expertise or attention.

- **E-Tasks**: Ever found yourself organizing your bookshelf when you have an impending deadline? Such tasks, while comforting, don't hold much water in the grand scheme of things. They can be eliminated or pushed back without any palpable loss. Activities like aimlessly scrolling through social media or re-arranging your desk for the umpteenth time often fall here.

The brilliance of the ABCDE method lies in its clarity. Instead of staring at a daunting list and wondering where to start, this approach provides a crystal-clear path. It implores us to confront our tasks, evaluate their worth, and then act in a manner that ensures we're always on top of our game, both in terms of efficiency and effectiveness. Adopting this method is akin to having a roadmap for productivity, guiding us through the terrains of responsibility with ease and purpose.

In summary, while tasks may seem insurmountable in their vastness, employing tailored prioritization techniques like the 2-Minute Rule, the Pareto Principle, and the ABCDE Method can transform the daunting into the doable. With these techniques in our arsenal, we are equipped to navigate the seas of responsibilities with purpose and precision.

CHAPTER 4

Calendar Management

Navigating the terrain of our daily commitments necessitates a structured framework, and this is where adept calendar management emerges as the linchpin. Far from being just a tool to remember birthdays or meeting schedules, a well-managed calendar becomes the roadmap of our intentions, translating our priorities into tangible time blocks. It stands as a reflection of not just where our time goes, but also where our priorities lie.

Appointments & Meetings

At a glance, calendars seem to be mere grids of dates, a simple tool for tracking days. But in reality, they're dynamic blueprints of our lives, capturing not just what we need to do, but also painting a picture of our priorities, our commitments, and the way we manage our time. In a world rife with responsibilities, an effectively managed calendar can be the difference between productive days and chaotic ones.

Set Reminders: We've all had those moments—realizing halfway through a day that we missed a crucial meeting or forgetting a friend's birthday until a belated social media notification reminds us. Enter the magic of reminders. Modern digital tools have revolutionized the way we interact with our calendars. By setting multiple reminders, not only do we ensure punctuality, but we're also mentally primed for the activity ahead. For example, if you have a presentation, a reminder a day before gives you time for a final review, while a second reminder an hour prior allows you to gather necessary materials. If you're catching a flight, reminders can be the cue to check-in, ensuring a smoother travel experience.

Allocate Buffer Time: Have you ever been in back-to-back meetings, rushing from one to the other, harried and not quite present because the previous one ran late? Such situations underscore the importance of buffer time. It's not just about accounting for overruns; it's about giving ourselves breathing space. If you've scheduled a lunch date right after a meeting, having a buffer ensures you're not keeping someone waiting because your meeting stretched a bit. Moreover, life is unpredictable—traffic delays, technological hitches, or just the simple need for a bathroom break. By integrating buffer time, you're factoring in life's little uncertainties, ensuring they don't throw your entire schedule off-kilter. For instance, if you're moving from a team meeting in the conference room to a client call in your office, that buffer might be the few minutes you need to gather your thoughts, grab a glass of water, and transition mentally.

In essence, calendars, when used adeptly, morph from mere tracking tools to strategic planners, ensuring our days are not just full, but meaningfully full. They become our silent allies in time management, ensuring that amidst the cacophony of commitments, we remain harmoniously tuned to our priorities.

Blocking Time for Tasks

Amidst a whirlwind of daily tasks and to-dos, there's a technique that stands out in its ability to transform chaos into structured productivity: Time-Blocking. This method extends the traditional use of calendars from just noting down meetings or appointments to meticulously carving out dedicated slots for individual tasks. Especially for those important tasks that often get side-lined because they aren't screaming for immediate attention- the Quadrant II tasks- time-blocking can be a lifesaver.

Prioritize Tasks: Just like a sculptor carefully chisels away, prioritizing tasks allows us to remove the unnecessary and focus on what truly adds value. But how do we decide what's paramount? By drawing upon techniques like the Pareto Principle, which reminds us that a significant chunk of our results often come from a fraction of our efforts. Or the ABCDE method, which ranks tasks based on their impact. Let's say you've recognized that strategizing for an upcoming campaign (a B-task) is more vital than replying to all emails (a C-task). By time-blocking, you ensure that campaign planning gets a dedicated slot in your calendar.

Allocate Uninterrupted Blocks: Picture this: you're in the zone, ideas are flowing, and just then, a notification pops up, breaking your flow. Distractions are productivity's nemesis. Especially for tasks demanding deep work or concentration, it's crucial to allocate extended, uninterrupted blocks. If you're a morning person and your creativity peaks then, block that time for high-focus tasks like writing or designing. This approach ensures that your best energy is spent on tasks that matter most, like preparing a vital presentation without the constant pings of email notifications.

Use Color Coding: A splash of color can make a world of difference. Think of your calendar as a canvas. By using different hues for various activities, at a glance, you can gauge the rhythm of your day. For instance, use green for brainstorming sessions, blue for administrative tasks, and red for meetings. This color differentiation not only makes your calendar visually appealing but also serves as a mental cue. If you see too much red (meetings) and not enough green (brainstorming or creative time), it might be a sign to recalibrate and ensure you're not stuck in back-to-back meetings at the cost of innovation.

To sum up, time-blocking is more than a calendaring technique. It's a commitment to yourself, ensuring that each day aligns with your priorities, enabling a blend of creativity, productivity, and well-deserved breaks. It's the bridge between intent and action, ensuring what we plan is precisely what we execute.

Consistency is Key

In the realm of time management, a calendar is akin to a ship's compass, guiding us through the vast sea of tasks and commitments. But like any instrument, its effectiveness hinges on its consistent use. Without regular check-ins and updates, even the most meticulously planned calendar can quickly become obsolete, leading us astray.

Daily Review: Think of this as your daily ritual, akin to brushing your teeth or having your morning coffee. Just as you wouldn't start your day without brushing away the night's sleep, similarly, a few minutes with your calendar can sweep away uncertainties, setting the tone for a productive day. Let's say you have a critical meeting tomorrow that you had forgotten about. A quick daily review the night before reminds you of this, allowing you to prepare and gather necessary materials. Or perhaps you notice a friend's birthday on the calendar during your morning review, giving you just enough time to send a thoughtful message or make a call. These daily touchpoints with your calendar serve as both reminders and reassurance, ensuring you're always a step ahead.

Weekly Planning: As the weekend approaches and the hustle and bustle of the week wind down, it's the perfect time to pull back and get a bird's eye view of the week ahead. Consider this your strategy session. Just as a general wouldn't go into battle without a plan, similarly, diving into a new week without a clear roadmap can lead to chaos. This isn't just about ensuring there's no overlap in appointments or double-bookings. It's about proactively carving out time for tasks that align with your broader goals. For instance, you've been meaning to start a new online course. During your weekly planning, you can block out dedicated study hours, turning intention into action. Moreover, life is full of surprises.

That unscheduled call or unexpected errand will crop up. By keeping some slots free during your weekly planning, you allow yourself the flexibility to navigate these unforeseen tasks without derailing your entire schedule.

In essence, consistent calendar management isn't just about recording tasks or meetings. It's about staying attuned to our commitments, both to ourselves and others, ensuring that each day and week unfolds with purpose, clarity, and direction.

Flexibility in Rigidity

In our quest for optimal time management, a calendar acts as a blueprint, outlining the day's structure. However, just like a sailor adjusting sails to changing winds, we must recognize the need for flexibility in our plans. A rigid calendar might offer the illusion of control, but life's unpredictability often throws a wrench into the most well-laid plans.

Keep Some Open Slots: Picture this: you've scheduled your day down to the last minute, ensuring every task and meeting has its dedicated slot. But midday, an unexpected client call runs over, eating into the time allocated for the next task. Now, the rest of the day's schedule cascades into chaos, each task delayed, leading to frustration and stress. Now, imagine a different scenario: the same overrun happens, but you've kept a few open slots in your calendar. These act as a cushion, absorbing such unexpected overruns and ensuring the rest of the day remains relatively unaffected. Besides unforeseen delays, these open slots can also offer moments of respite—a chance to stretch, grab a cup of coffee, or simply gather your thoughts. In a world that glorifies back-to-back scheduling, such intentional breaks can be game-changers for mental well-being.

Re-evaluate and Adjust: Let's take the example of a monthly report you're responsible for at work. You've always allocated two hours for it, but for the past three months, it's been consistently taking three. Instead of merely adjusting your calendar to allocate more time, it's crucial to dive deeper. Is the report's scope broader now? Are there new data sources you're integrating, adding to the time? Or perhaps it's a sign that the task itself has become more complex, warranting a discussion about resources or delegation. Adjusting time blocks is not just about moving slots around. It's an opportunity to understand task evolution and ensure that your calendar remains a reflection of the true time investment tasks require.

In conclusion, while calendars are crucial for effective time management, they shouldn't be viewed as immutable laws. Recognizing the fluid nature of our lives and building in mechanisms to adjust to this flux ensures that our calendar remains a tool for productivity, not a source of pressure.

Embracing Adaptability in Calendar Management

In the ever-evolving landscape of our personal and professional lives, calendars stand as sentinels of structure. These tools, far beyond their basic function of marking dates, hold the potential to be a reflection of our priorities, intentions, and aspirations. But for calendars to truly serve us, two key elements must be upheld: consistency in updating and flexibility in execution.

Consistency is Key:

Daily Review: Integrating a daily calendar review into your routine can be as rejuvenating as your morning cup of coffee. It not only sets the day's tone but also ensures that no task or commitment slips through the cracks. For instance, a cursory evening review might remind you of a morning meeting, allowing you to prepare overnight and hit the ground running the next day. It's like laying out your clothes the night before, ensuring a smoother start.

Weekly Planning: Just as a chef preps for the week ahead, ensuring all ingredients are in place, a weekly look at your calendar is your prep time. This is your moment to strategize, ensuring that the tasks align with your broader goals. For instance, if you've been meaning to start a fitness routine, this is when you carve out dedicated slots for workouts, transforming aspirations into actionable steps. This ritual also ensures a balance between work, personal commitments, and the all-important 'me time'.

Flexibility in Rigidity:

Keep Some Open Slots: Consider the scenario where a business meeting unexpectedly extends into your lunch break, throwing the day's schedule into disarray. Having buffer or open slots in your calendar is like having airbags in a car—they cushion unexpected impacts. These slots can absorb unplanned tasks or simply provide a mental and physical breather. It's akin to keeping a small savings stash for unexpected expenses. The knowledge that you have this buffer provides peace of mind and the agility to adapt.

Re-evaluate and Adjust: Tasks evolve. A monthly report that once took two hours might now, with added data or complexity, take three. Rather than forcibly fit it into the old time slot, it's crucial to reassess. This might mean allocating more time or even redefining the task itself. This isn't merely about shuffling time blocks but is a more profound exercise in understanding the evolving nature of responsibilities.

In summing up, the essence of effective calendar management is rooted in a harmonious blend of consistency and flexibility. While a calendar provides the scaffold, ensuring our days have structure and direction, our approach to it should be fluid, accommodating the inevitable ebb and flow of life. As we journey through our days, our calendar, if managed well, can be our compass, ensuring we stay true to our course, even amidst life's unpredictable storms.

CHAPTER 5

Alec Mackenzie's Time Trap

Time, as they say, waits for no one. And in our relentless pursuit to harness it, we often fall into certain pitfalls or 'traps' that seem innocuous but have significant cumulative effects on our productivity. Alec Mackenzie, in his work, identified these as "Time Traps". These are the common mistakes we make, often unknowingly, that fritter away our precious hours.

The 20 Time Traps:

1. **Attempting too Much**: The ambition to achieve can sometimes lead to overcommitting, leaving one feeling overwhelmed and exhausted. Example: Taking on multiple projects simultaneously can dilute focus and reduce overall effectiveness.

2. **Procrastination**: The act of continually postponing tasks that should be done immediately. This often leads to a backlog of work and unnecessary stress. Example: Pushing off a report until the last minute can result in rushed, subpar work.

3. **Lack of Self-Discipline**: Disregarding set guidelines or personal routines can lead to erratic work patterns. Example: Frequently sleeping past the set wake-up time can derail the day's schedule.

4. **Not Setting Personal Goals**: Without a clear objective or target, efforts can become unfocused and scattered. Example: Working in sales without a monthly target can lead to aimless effort.

5. **Failure to Prioritize**: Treating all tasks with equal weight can mean missing out on completing essential tasks. Example: Spending hours on emails while a project deadline looms.

6. **No Daily Planning**: Diving into the day without a clear agenda can result in reactive rather than proactive work. Example: Handling tasks randomly as they come up without assessing their importance.

7. **Poor Communication**: Ambiguous communication can lead to misalignment and rework. Example: Unclear instructions can cause team members to produce unintended results.

8. **Ineffective Delegation**: Either holding onto tasks that could be assigned or not giving clear instructions can stall progress. Example: A manager redoing a task instead of providing feedback.

9. **Meeting Mania**: Excessive meetings, especially those without clear agendas, can devour productive hours. Example: Holding daily team meetings where half the time is spent without direction.

10. **Tele-interruptions**: Consistent disturbances from phones or messaging apps can break concentration and workflow. Example: A deep focus task is interrupted by non-urgent phone calls.

11. **Lack of Organization**: A disordered workspace or workflow can hinder productivity and induce stress. Example: Wasting time searching for a document amidst a cluttered desk.

12. **Incomplete Information**: Starting tasks without adequate details can lead to pauses and inaccuracies. Example: Writing a report without all necessary data.

13. **Working in a Crisis Mode**: Being perpetually in a reactionary state can prevent strategic, forward-thinking work. Example: Addressing only urgent customer complaints without focusing on long-term solutions.

14. **Lack of Self-Training**: Failing to continuously update one's skills or knowledge can result in inefficiencies. Example: Using outdated software due to lack of training on the latest version.

15. **Inability to Say 'No'**: Overextending oneself due to an inability to set boundaries can reduce effectiveness. Example: Agreeing to all project requests without assessing bandwidth.

16. **Not Taking Breaks**: Continuous work without breaks can reduce mental sharpness and increase fatigue. Example: Working for five hours straight without a short break.

17. **Avoiding Difficult Tasks**: Shunning challenging but crucial tasks can result in last-minute pressures. Example: Avoiding difficult client conversations until issues escalate.

18. **Socializing Too Much**: While building relationships is vital, excessive non-work-related chats can eat into productive time. Example: Spending the first hour at work discussing a TV series.

19. **Not Reviewing Progress**: Neglecting to assess one's own progress can mean missing course correction opportunities. Example: Not checking progress on quarterly goals.

20. **Resistance to New Technology**: Avoiding new tools or technologies can mean missing out on efficiencies. Example: Sticking to manual data entry when automation tools are available.

Each of these traps, while seeming trivial in isolation, can collectively create significant barriers to effective time management. Recognizing them is the first step towards crafting solutions.

10 Techniques to Counter These Time Traps:

1. **Time Auditing**: Just as financial audits assess where money goes, time auditing evaluates how we spend our hours and minutes. By keeping a detailed log, perhaps for a week, we gain a clearer picture of our patterns, inefficiencies, and, most importantly, opportunities for improvement. For example, you might discover you're spending an inordinate amount of time on emails, pointing to a potential area for optimization.

2. **The Eisenhower Box**: This tool, rooted in Dwight D. Eisenhower's time management wisdom, bifurcates tasks based on urgency and importance. The magic lies in its simplicity: by classifying tasks within its four quadrants, we can immediately determine what needs immediate attention, what should be scheduled, what can be delegated, and what might be eliminated. For instance, a pressing deadline might fall into the "urgent and important" quadrant, demanding immediate focus.

3. **Set Clear Boundaries**: In the era of remote work and digital communication, boundaries can blur. By setting aside specific periods for work, breaks, and personal time, we respect our own mental space and allow for structured productivity. For example, having a "no meetings" block in the mid-morning might safeguard your peak productive hours.

4. **Use Technology**: In today's digital age, an array of tools exists to bolster efficiency. From project management software like Trello to distraction blockers like "Focus@Will", technology can be a formidable ally in time management. A practical instance might be using an app like "RescueTime" to gauge where your digital time goes.

5. **Continuous Learning**: The world evolves, and with it, new methods and techniques emerge. By committing to regular upskilling, not only do we enhance our professional value, but

we also arm ourselves with innovative strategies for efficiency. A marketing professional, for instance, might benefit from learning the latest in digital advertising trends.

6. **Delegate Effectively**: Delegation isn't about shirking responsibility but about maximizing team efficiency. By assigning tasks that align with team members' strengths and expertise, and trusting them to execute without micro-management, we foster both team growth and project efficiency. For instance, delegate a graphic design task to someone with that specific skill set rather than struggling through it yourself.

7. **Set SMART Goals**: Goals can be nebulous or concrete. SMART goals—those that are Specific, Measurable, Achievable, Relevant, and Time-bound—fall into the latter category. Such clarity ensures that we have a distinct path forward, with each step purposefully taking us closer to our objective. Instead of a vague "increase sales" goal, a SMART goal would be "increase sales by 10% in Q2."

8. **Establish Daily Routines**: Starting the day with purpose often sets the tone for the hours that follow. A structured morning routine, perhaps encompassing reading, exercise, and goal-setting, can lead to a more focused and productive day. For many, this might mean starting with a quiet meditation or journaling session.

9. **Limit Interruptions**: In an interconnected world, distractions are rife. By carving out specific times for emails, calls, or other potential disruptions, we ensure that our prime focus periods remain undisturbed. It might mean setting your messaging apps to "Do Not Disturb" during your peak work hours.

10. **Review and Reflect**: Progress thrives on feedback. By taking stock of our weeks—celebrating achievements, identifying snags, and plotting the course for the week ahead—we engage in a continuous cycle of improvement. This might look like a Friday evening session where you review the week's goals versus achievements and plan for the upcoming week.

Each of these techniques, when applied consciously, can incrementally lead to a transformation in how we manage our time, turning hours into assets rather than fleeting moments.

Mackenzie's "Time Traps" elucidates the pitfalls that can stealthily erode our productivity. By being aware of them and arming ourselves with the right techniques to counteract, we can navigate our workdays efficiently, ensuring each moment is spent judiciously.

CHAPTER 6

Time Boxing

Time Boxing: A Comprehensive Insight

In the vast landscape of time management techniques, one approach stands out both for its simplicity and its efficacy: Time Boxing.

Definition of Time Boxing: Time Boxing is a structured method where you allocate a predetermined amount of time, or "time box", for a specific task or set of tasks. Unlike traditional task-based approaches where you work on a task until it's finished, with Time Boxing, the focus is on the amount of time spent on the task rather than reaching completion. The aim is to dive deep into the task during this period, minimizing distractions and maximizing efficiency.

Descriptive Insight: Picture a boxing ring where, instead of rounds of physical combat, you have rounds of focused work. The bell rings, signaling the start, and you dive into the task at hand, giving it your undivided attention. Another bell chimes at the end of the round, indicating it's time to step back. This isn't about racing against the clock, but rather maximizing the quality of time spent on the task. It operates on the principle that dedicated bursts of concentration can often be more productive than prolonged periods of divided attention.

The Practicality Behind Time Boxing: The logic is twofold. Firstly, knowing that there's a defined end time can serve as a motivator, pushing you to work more diligently. It removes the open-endedness that can often lead to procrastination. Secondly, by working in these focused sprints, it's easier to maintain peak concentration and prevent burnout.

Example: Consider the task of checking emails, which many often find endless. Without a structured approach, you could find yourself spending hours getting lost in threads, only to emerge feeling like the day has slipped away. Now, apply the time boxing method. Allocate, for instance, 30 minutes in the morning to this task. During this half-hour, your sole focus is emails. You don't entertain distractions, and you approach this with the intent of maximizing this time frame. When the 30 minutes are up, you move on, regardless of whether you've reached the mythical "inbox zero" or not. The goal was not to finish your emails but to dedicate 30 focused minutes to them.

Practical Tips for Effective Time Boxing:

1. **Be Realistic**: If you allocate 15 minutes for a task that realistically takes an hour, you're setting yourself up for failure. Start by gauging how long tasks typically take and then allocate time boxes accordingly.

2. **Use Tools**: There are numerous digital timers and apps designed specifically for time boxing. Tools like the Pomodoro Technique, where you work for 25 minutes followed by a 5-minute break, can be particularly effective.

3. **Limit Distractions**: The essence of time boxing is focused work. Ensure your workspace is conducive to this. This might mean putting your phone on airplane mode or using apps that block distracting sites.

4. **Flexibility**: While the essence of time boxing is to stick to the allocated time, there will be occasions where extending a time box is necessary. Use your judgment, but be wary of consistently overextending.

5. **Review and Adjust**: At the end of the week, review your tasks. Were the time boxes realistic? Were tasks completed in the allocated time? Adjust your time boxes based on this reflection for the next week.

6. **Incorporate Breaks**: Never underestimate the power of short breaks between time boxes. They provide an opportunity to stretch, hydrate, and refresh, ensuring you approach the next time box with renewed vigor.

In essence, Time Boxing is more than just a time management technique; it's a philosophy that encourages concentrated work and celebrates the quality of time over quantity. It recognizes that in our distraction-prone world, the true value lies in focused bursts of undivided attention. By setting clear boundaries for tasks, we're not only more efficient but also gain a greater sense of accomplishment and control over our workday.

Tools and Techniques for Effective Time Boxing

Time Boxing, a powerful method for enhancing productivity, is further augmented by an array of tools and techniques designed to streamline and optimize the process. These tools, ranging from digital applications to traditional methods, aim to structure your work sessions, ensuring that you maximize each time box's potential.

1. Digital Timers:

Description: Digital timers, accessible on smartphones, tablets, or computers, allow users to set precise time intervals for their tasks. Unlike traditional clocks, these timers offer customization options such as different alarm tones, vibrations, or visual signals.

Usage: Set your timer for the duration of your chosen time box, let's say 30 minutes. Work diligently on your task until the timer sounds, signaling the end of that focused work period. Many digital timers also allow you to set interval reminders, so if you want a heads-up 5 minutes before your time ends, you can program it in.

2. Dedicated Time Boxing Apps:

Description: There's a plethora of applications designed specifically for time boxing. These apps often come with enhanced features, such as tracking your completed time boxes, providing statistics on your work patterns, or even offering reward systems.

Usage: Apps like 'Be Focused', 'Focus Keeper', and 'Toggl' enable users to not only set their time boxes but also categorize tasks, ensuring that over time, you gain insights into where your time is most productively spent.

3. Traditional Alarms and Timers:

Description: For those who prefer a more tactile approach or wish to reduce screen time, traditional alarms and kitchen timers can be effective. The ringing of a traditional bell can be a more assertive cue to end a work session than a digital beep.

Usage: If you're using a traditional alarm clock, set the alarm for the end of your work period. With kitchen timers, twist the timer to your desired duration and get to work. The physical act of setting the time can also reinforce commitment to the task.

4. Color-Coded Time Blocks:

Description: Visual learners and organizers might benefit from color-coding their time boxes. Using different colors for various tasks can give a quick overview of the day's activities and ensure a balanced work schedule.

Usage: On digital calendars like Google Calendar or Microsoft Outlook, allocate different colors for different tasks. For instance, blue for deep work, red for meetings, and green for creative brainstorming. A glance at your calendar provides instant clarity on the day's structure.

5. Task Management Software with Time Boxing Features:

Description: Platforms like Trello, Asana, or Monday.com, primarily used for task management, often come with built-in time boxing features or allow integrations with time boxing apps.

Usage: When setting up a task in these platforms, use their time boxing or timer features to allocate specific time durations to each task. This way, your task list and time boxes are integrated, providing a comprehensive overview of your workload.

In conclusion, while the concept of Time Boxing is straightforward, its effectiveness can be substantially enhanced using the right tools and techniques. Whether you're a digital native who thrives with apps or someone who prefers the tangibility of traditional timers, there's a tool out there tailored for your needs. The key is to find the one that resonates with you and integrate it into your daily routine, ensuring your work sessions are both productive and structured.

Benefits

1. Increased Focus:

- **Benefit Explanation**: One of the significant challenges in today's hyper-connected world is maintaining consistent focus on a given task. Distractions are incessant, from the pings of social media notifications to the lure of a quick online article. However, with the implementation of time boxing, this dynamic shifts. By allocating a specific, non-negotiable duration for a task, our minds are conditioned to understand that there's only a limited window to accomplish it. This creates a psychological contract of sorts– a commitment to give undivided attention to the task at hand. The fixed timeframe serves as a shield against potential distractions, ushering in a heightened sense of purpose and a laser-sharp focus.

- **Impact**: The direct consequence of this increased focus is not just faster task completion but also improved quality of work. When our attention isn't fractured by constant diversions, the depth and quality of our engagement with the task are significantly enhanced. This not only boosts productivity but also instills a sense of accomplishment and satisfaction. Over time, this focused approach can lead to honing skills faster, achieving goals with more efficiency, and even fostering a more profound sense of professional fulfillment.

- **Example for Clarification**: Consider a scenario where you're working on a crucial project presentation. The deadline is looming, but so is the allure of your buzzing phone with social media updates, or perhaps the inviting aroma of coffee. By employing time boxing and deciding that the next hour will be solely devoted to the presentation, you mentally bracket out these temptations. You're fully aware that after the allocated hour, you can indulge in a break. This mindset significantly diminishes the temptation to wander off-task, ensuring that the hour is spent in genuine, productive work on the project.

2. Prevents Burnout:

Benefit Explanation: Burnout is an all-too-familiar term in contemporary work cultures. It represents the exhaustion and overwhelming feeling that arises from prolonged periods of stress and excessive workloads. Time boxing, by its very nature, is a preventive measure against burnout. By setting strict boundaries on how long you'll work on a task, you're ensuring that you don't get so engrossed that you lose track of time and overextend yourself. These boundaries foster a rhythm of work and rest, ensuring that energy reserves are maintained and replenished.

Impact: The consistent pauses and breaks that time boxing integrates into one's day ensure that the brain and body get necessary intervals of rest. This not only maintains consistent energy levels but also aids in mental clarity, creativity, and problem-solving abilities. Over the longer term, this balanced approach to work reduces the risk of chronic stress, health issues, and burnout, leading to sustainable productivity and a healthier work-life balance.

Example for Clarification: Imagine you're a content writer, and you have three articles to draft in one day. Without boundaries, you might find yourself working non-stop, trying to perfect one piece, consuming hours, and leaving little energy for the others. By time boxing, say, two hours per article, you're ensuring that you give focused attention to each without draining all your energy on just one. After each two-hour block, a break allows for relaxation, perhaps a walk or some light reading, before diving into the next task. This rhythm ensures that by day's end, you've worked efficiently on all three articles without feeling completely drained or overwhelmed.

Challenges

1. Potential for Incompletion:

- **Explanation**: One of the significant challenges of time boxing is the risk of underestimating the duration a task might require. When setting a specific block of time for a task, there's an underlying assumption about how long that task will take. This estimation, especially if done without prior experience or data, can often be off-mark. As a result, when the time box ends, the task might still be incomplete, leading to potential disruptions in the workflow, stress over unfinished work, and the need to either extend the time box (which might affect other tasks) or resume it later.

- **How It Affects Outcome**: Incompletion can have a ripple effect. Not finishing a task within its designated time can lead to feelings of inadequacy or frustration. Additionally, it can offset the schedule for subsequent tasks or commitments. Regular instances of incompletion can also diminish trust in the time boxing method itself, leading individuals to either abandon the approach or become demotivated. In professional settings, consistent incompletion might also lead to missed deadlines or commitments, impacting credibility.

- **Example for Explanation**: Consider a scenario where you're prepping for a meeting. Based on initial assessment, you time box 15 minutes to review the agenda and gather necessary documents. However, as you delve into the task, you realize that one of the topics is more complex than anticipated and requires a deeper dive. Before you know it, the 15-minute timer goes off, and you've only covered half of what you intended. Now, you're faced with a dilemma: Do you extend the time and risk pushing other tasks? Or do you move on and potentially be underprepared for the meeting? This situation exemplifies the challenge of potential incompletion due to time underestimation.

2. Rigidity:

- **Explanation**: Time boxing, by design, is a structured approach. Each task is fitted into a neatly defined timeframe, providing clarity and focus. However, this rigidity might not always be advantageous. Certain tasks, especially those that are creative or exploratory in nature, might not always conform to strict time boundaries. These tasks often require a state of 'flow', where the individual is deeply immersed, and creativity is at its peak. Introducing rigid time limits can disrupt this flow, curtailing creativity and potentially affecting the quality of the output.

- **How It Affects Outcome**: The strict nature of time boxing can sometimes be counterproductive, especially for tasks that thrive on flexibility. By cutting short a flow state, the end product might lack depth, creativity, or thoroughness. Moreover, for individuals who naturally lean towards a more flexible, organic working style, the rigidity of time boxing can feel constraining, leading to decreased motivation or job satisfaction.

- **Example for Explanation**: Imagine a graphic designer working on a new logo design. She enters a state of deep immersion, experimenting with colors, shapes, and typography. Just as she's on the verge of a breakthrough idea, her timer signals the end of her time box. Now she's forced to either break her flow and move to the next task or adjust her schedule to accommodate her creative process. This scenario highlights how the rigidity of time boxing might not always be conducive to tasks that require unhindered exploration and creativity.

Summary

Time boxing is an effective time management technique where specific time intervals are designated for particular tasks or activities. The objective is to accomplish as much of the task as possible within the set period, promoting efficiency and focus.

The approach has notable benefits:

1. **Increased Focus**: Setting a fixed time reduces the potential for distractions and imbues the task at hand with a heightened sense of purpose. For instance, if you're aware that you only have an hour for a project, you're more likely to stay engaged and resist diversions like checking social media.

2. **Prevents Burnout**: By providing clear boundaries on the duration of a task, time boxing prevents overexertion on a single activity, ensuring energy conservation for subsequent tasks. For

example, setting specific time limits for work tasks means there's also intentional downtime, fostering a balanced day.

However, there are challenges to this method:

1. **Potential for Incompletion**: There's a risk of not finishing a task if the time allocated is underestimated. For example, dedicating just 15 minutes for a task that realistically needs 30 minutes can result in unfinished work, leading to disruptions and potential stress.

2. **Rigidity**: Time boxing's strict nature might not be suitable for all tasks or all individuals. Tasks that require a flow state, like certain creative endeavors, might not thrive within constrained time limits.

Various tools, from digital timers to specific apps, can assist in implementing time boxing. One popular technique is the Pomodoro Technique, where tasks are broken down into 25-minute focused intervals, followed by a 5-minute break.

In conclusion, time boxing offers a structured approach to managing tasks, balancing the benefits of increased focus and prevention of burnout with the challenges of potential incompletion and rigidity. Properly used, it can be a transformative technique in time management.

CHAPTER 7

Pomodoro Technique

Francesco Cirillo's Method of Breaking Work into Intervals

In the realms of time management and productivity, myriad techniques claim to offer the ultimate path to enhanced focus and efficiency. Among these, the Pomodoro Technique, conceived by Francesco Cirillo, stands out for its simplicity and effectiveness.

Background:

Introduction to Francesco Cirillo:

Francesco Cirillo, an Italian developer and entrepreneur, crafted this technique during the late 1980s. While he was a university student, Cirillo was searching for a way to optimize his study habits and make the most out of his time. Like many students, he faced the common challenges of distractions, procrastination, and the feeling of being overwhelmed by the vastness of assignments and responsibilities.

The Inception and Inspiration for the Pomodoro Technique:

The solution he stumbled upon was disarmingly simple: a kitchen timer shaped like a tomato. By using this timer to break his work into focused intervals, Cirillo found that he could maintain his concentration and drive, turning the intimidating ocean of tasks into a series of manageable streams. Thus, the Pomodoro Technique was born. The name "Pomodoro" pays homage to the Italian word for tomato, a nod to the original tomato-shaped timer Cirillo used during his experimentation.

Core Concept:

Explanation of the Pomodoro Intervals:

The foundational principle of the Pomodoro Technique is to divide work into chunks, or "pomodoros," of focused activity. The standard recommendation is a 25-minute work session. This duration was chosen after Cirillo's experimentation, as it represents a balance—long enough to dive deep into a task, yet short enough to maintain high energy and focus. Following each pomodoro, a short break, typically 5 minutes, is taken. This brief interlude serves multiple purposes: it offers the brain a moment of respite, allows for physical movement, and provides an opportunity to reset and prepare for the next task.

Significance of the term 'Pomodoro':

While the term 'Pomodoro' might initially evoke thoughts of Italian cuisine, in this context, it symbolizes more than just a tomato. It represents the idea of time: finite, yet renewable. Each tomato or pomodoro is a self-contained unit of productivity. The consistent and repetitive use of the timer serves as a tactile and auditory reminder of the technique's principles, reinforcing the cyclical nature of the work-break pattern.

Extended Breaks After Every Fourth Pomodoro:

The Pomodoro Technique is not just about alternating between work and short breaks. After completing four consecutive pomodoros, a longer break, often 15-30 minutes, is recommended. This extended pause is crucial for several reasons. Firstly, it offers an opportunity for deeper relaxation and recuperation, allowing for both mental and physical detangling from work. Secondly, it acts as a reward, a mini-celebration of the progress made during the four pomodoros. Lastly, this longer break ensures that the brain isn't pushed to a point of diminishing returns, where fatigue could begin compromising the quality of work.

In essence, the Pomodoro Technique, birthed from the quest of a university student trying to harness his time and focus, has grown into a globally recognized methodology, helping countless individuals navigate their professional and personal tasks. By segmenting time, emphasizing regular breaks, and using a tangible timer (whether it's a tomato-shaped one or a digital app), this technique transforms the abstract concept of "time" into concrete, manageable intervals, ushering in an era of structured productivity.

Benefits of the Pomodoro Technique

In today's fast-paced world, the challenge of optimizing productivity while ensuring mental well-being remains ever-present. Amidst the cacophony of various time management techniques, the Pomodoro Technique emerges as a beacon, offering a harmonious blend of focus, efficiency, and balance. The benefits of this method are manifold, ranging from enhanced productivity to the prevention of burnout.

Increased Productivity:

How Time Constraints Create a Sense of Urgency and Reduce Procrastination: One of the primary virtues of the Pomodoro Technique lies in its imposition of time constraints. By setting a definitive start and end to work intervals, it instills a sense of urgency. The ticking clock serves as a reminder that time is fleeting, motivating individuals to maximize their output within the 25-minute window. This artificial constraint acts as a deterrent to procrastination. When faced with a sprawling, unstructured day, the temptation to delay tasks is significant. However, when the day is compartmentalized into a series of pomodoros, the mindset shifts from "I have all day to do this" to "I have 25 minutes to make as much progress as possible."

The Psychological Rewards of Completing Tasks Within Time Intervals: Beyond the tangible progress made during each pomodoro, there lies a psychological reward system. Completing a task or a portion of it within the stipulated time offers a dopamine hit, a sense of achievement. This fosters motivation. The act of physically winding down the timer or marking the completion of a pomodoro can be immensely satisfying, propelling the individual to dive into the next task with renewed vigor.

Enhanced Focus:

The Reduction of Distractions by Committing to Short, Focused Work Periods: The modern work environment is riddled with distractions, from the incessant ping of notifications to the allure of social media. The Pomodoro Technique, with its emphasis on undivided attention for short bursts, becomes an antidote to these distractions. Committing to just 25 minutes of focused work becomes psychologically manageable. The implicit understanding is that after this period, one can attend to other distractions, making it easier to resist them during the pomodoro.

The Positive Cycle: Improved Concentration Leading to More Completed Pomodoros: As individuals immerse themselves in the rhythm of the Pomodoro Technique, a positive feedback loop emerges. With each successful, distraction-free pomodoro, the ability to concentrate improves. This heightened focus leads to more tasks being accomplished within subsequent pomodoros, reinforcing the technique's efficacy and encouraging its continued adoption.

Structured Breaks:

The Importance of Allowing the Brain to Rest and Rejuvenate: While the work intervals in the Pomodoro Technique are integral, the breaks in between are equally, if not more, vital. Our brains aren't designed to maintain unwavering focus for extended periods. These structured breaks offer moments of respite, allowing the brain to reset. Activities like stretching, taking a quick walk, or even just deep breathing during these intervals provide the necessary mental rejuvenation.

How Regular Breaks Can Prevent Burnout and Mental Fatigue: The consequences of relentless work without breaks are well-documented: burnout, decreased productivity, and a decline in mental well-being. The Pomodoro Technique, with its embedded breaks, serves as a bulwark against such outcomes. By ensuring that work is punctuated with regular intervals of rest, it fosters sustainability. The brain remains fresh, ideas flow more freely, and the onset of mental fatigue is delayed.

In summary, the Pomodoro Technique isn't merely a time management strategy; it's a holistic approach to work. By intertwining focused work periods with deliberate breaks, it not only amplifies productivity but also champions the importance of mental well-being, making it a quintessential tool for the modern professional.

Best Practices for the Pomodoro Technique

The efficacy of the Pomodoro Technique isn't merely in its fundamental principles but in how they're adapted and applied to one's personal workflow. To extract the most value from this time management system, here are some best practices, from tool selection to managing inevitable interruptions.

Tool Selection:

Traditional timers vs. digital Pomodoro apps: When Francesco Cirillo devised the Pomodoro Technique, he used a simple tomato-shaped kitchen timer, which later gave the method its iconic name. Today, while the allure of the tactile experience of winding up a mechanical timer remains for some, digital advancements have provided a myriad of alternatives. Digital Pomodoro apps offer features beyond mere timing—analytics, integration with other productivity tools, and customizable time intervals, to name a few. However, the choice between traditional and digital depends on one's personal preference. Some find the ticking sound of a mechanical timer therapeutic, providing a constant reminder of passing time, while others prefer the silent countdown of digital versions.

Recommendations for reliable Pomodoro tools and apps: For those leaning towards digital, apps like 'Focus Keeper', 'TomatoTimer', and 'PomoDoneApp' come highly recommended. They offer a mix of intuitive design, customizability, and, in some cases, integration with task management tools. However, for purists who want to experience the technique in its most authentic form, any traditional kitchen timer will do.

Environment Setup:

Creating a conducive work environment free of distractions: The Pomodoro Technique's efficacy is magnified in an environment optimized for focus. This involves eliminating potential distractions—putting your phone on airplane mode, closing irrelevant browser tabs, or using apps like 'Cold Turkey' or 'Freedom' to block distracting websites. Ambient noise can be another concern. If you're in a noisy environment, consider noise-canceling headphones or apps that play white noise or calming sounds.

Having all materials and resources ready before starting a Pomodoro: A significant aspect of maintaining flow during a pomodoro is ensuring you have all the resources at hand before you begin. This could mean having all relevant research materials open, ensuring necessary software or tools are operational, or even something as simple as having a notepad and pen ready for jotting down thoughts. This proactive preparation prevents the disruption of your workflow once the timer starts ticking.

Managing Interruptions:

Tips on how to handle unexpected interruptions: No matter how well you prepare, interruptions are often inevitable. When faced with one, a useful strategy is to employ the 'inform, negotiate, and call back' method. First, inform the interrupter that you're in the middle of something. Then, negotiate a specific time when you'll get back to them. Finally, ensure you do circle back at the agreed-upon time.

Strategies for rescheduling or integrating urgent tasks into the Pomodoro workflow: There will be instances when an urgent task crops up in the middle of a pomodoro. In such cases, it's vital to make a quick assessment. If the task can wait until the end of the pomodoro, jot it down and attend to it during the break. If it's genuinely pressing, stop the pomodoro, address the urgent task, and then reset the timer. The key is flexibility, without allowing every minor interruption to derail the pomodoro.

In essence, the Pomodoro Technique, while powerful, thrives on customization. The timer, be it digital or traditional, is merely a tool; the true value lies in creating an environment and mindset optimized for focus and productivity. By tailoring the method to individual needs and equipping oneself with strategies to manage the unpredictable, one can truly harness the transformative power of the Pomodoro Technique.

Customization in the Pomodoro Technique

The Pomodoro Technique, developed by Francesco Cirillo in the late 1980s, fundamentally prescribes 25-minute work intervals, known as 'pomodoros', punctuated by short breaks. However, as with any productivity method, the Pomodoro Technique's power isn't just in its original blueprint but in its adaptability to individual preferences and the variety of tasks we encounter in modern work environments.

Adjusting the Length of Work Intervals and Breaks:

The primary allure of the Pomodoro Technique is its simplicity, but the one-size-fits-all approach might not resonate with everyone. While 25 minutes of focused work followed by a 5-minute break works for many, others might find this timing too constricting or too lax, depending on the task at hand or their personal productivity rhythms.

Some individuals find that tasks requiring deep concentration—such as writing, programming, or design—benefit from longer periods of undisturbed focus. Extending the pomodoro to 50 minutes, followed by a 10-minute break, might be more appropriate for these individuals. Conversely, tasks that are mentally exhausting or tedious might benefit from shorter bursts of effort. For instance, tasks like data entry or sorting might be tackled more effectively in 15-minute intervals with 3-4 minute breaks.

Guidelines for Determining When to Modify the Traditional 25-Minute Work Period:

1. **Understand Your Natural Rhythm:** Everyone has their rhythm of productivity—some people can maintain intense focus for longer periods, while others work best in short, sharp bursts. Observing when your concentration starts to wane during a task can give insights into your optimal work period. For instance, if you consistently find yourself distracted 20 minutes into a task, it might be beneficial to shorten your work interval.

2. **Task Complexity and Nature:** Not all tasks are created equal. Deep work tasks, such as research, complex problem-solving, or creative endeavors, might benefit from longer, uninterrupted

focus. In contrast, routine or repetitive tasks might be more manageable in shorter bursts, preventing them from becoming overly monotonous.

3. **Experiment and Reflect:** Consider tweaking the traditional pomodoro duration as an experiment. If you're contemplating extending the work period, try a 40-minute interval with an 8-minute break. After a few cycles, reflect on whether you felt more productive and if the longer interval enhanced or hindered your focus.

4. **Mind Your Energy Levels:** Our energy isn't consistent throughout the day. Some people are most alert in the morning, while others hit their stride in the evening. If you're a morning person, you might be able to handle longer pomodoros early in the day, reverting to shorter intervals as the day progresses and energy levels dip.

5. **Break Quality Matters:** If you're adjusting your work intervals, it's essential to adjust your breaks correspondingly. These intervals aren't just about physical rest but mental rejuvenation. If you're working for 50 minutes, a 5-minute break might not suffice. Use this time effectively—stretch, take deep breaths, or even engage in a short mindfulness exercise. The goal is to return to the next interval mentally refreshed.

6. **Avoid Burnout:** It's essential to ensure that in the pursuit of productivity, you don't push yourself too hard. If you're consistently feeling exhausted or finding the quality of your work diminishing, it might be a sign that your intervals are too long without adequate rest.

In conclusion, the Pomodoro Technique's foundational principle is structured work and rest intervals. While the traditional 25-minute period offers a starting point, the technique's true potency lies in its adaptability. By tuning into one's preferences, understanding the nature of tasks, and being willing to experiment and adjust, one can mold the Pomodoro Technique to be a truly personalized productivity powerhouse.

CHAPTER 8

The Time Management Process

E ffective time management is a jigsaw puzzle, where each piece represents a different technique, tool, or principle. When you master the art of fitting these pieces together, you create a comprehensive picture of productivity. This chapter delves into synthesizing the techniques and principles discussed in the previous chapters to build a holistic time management routine tailored to individual needs.

Understanding the Significance of Time Management:

Time management, a term often bandied about in both professional and personal contexts, is not just about ticking off tasks on a to-do list. To genuinely appreciate its importance, one needs to delve deeper into the reasons that underscore its relevance in our lives.

The first point of inquiry is the very nature of time. It remains one of life's most egalitarian resources; every individual, irrespective of background, wealth, or status, has the same 24 hours in a day. How we choose to allocate these hours, minutes, and seconds plays a pivotal role in determining the quality of our lives. This is where the essence of time management comes into play.

Let's address the primary misconception: time management is solely about productivity. While boosting productivity is a significant outcome, time management transcends this. It's about orchestrating our days in such a manner that we derive genuine value and satisfaction from the tasks we undertake. Be it a project at work, spending time with family, or pursuing a hobby, managing time ensures we give due attention to activities that resonate with our core values and aspirations.

Maintaining a work-life balance is another critical facet illuminated by effective time management. In an era where the lines between professional and personal lives are increasingly blurred, especially with remote work scenarios, managing time becomes the compass that helps navigate these overlapping domains. It ensures that work doesn't perpetually overshadow personal moments, and vice versa.

Reducing stress is an often-underestimated benefit. A chaotic day, characterized by missed deadlines and overlapping commitments, can be a significant source of anxiety. Time management, by providing a structured framework, diminishes the chaos, making tasks and commitments more manageable. It offers clarity, allowing individuals to tackle challenges methodically rather than reactively.

Moreover, aligning our days with personal and professional goals can't be understated. Time management acts as the bridge connecting our daily activities with long-term objectives. Each task, when viewed through the lens of time management, becomes a step towards a broader goal, adding purpose and direction to our actions.

Lastly, the overarching impact of effective time management is the enhancement of life satisfaction. When we manage our time well, we're not just optimizing our days; we're optimizing our lives. We ensure that our time, our most finite resource, is invested in endeavors that bring fulfillment, growth, and happiness.

Understanding the true significance of time management requires a holistic perspective. It's not just a tool for efficiency but a philosophy that, when embraced, enriches every facet of our lives, grounding our days in purpose and intention.

Assessing Your Current Time Management Habits:

Time management, in its essence, is a continuous process of understanding, evaluating, and refining. Before one can effectively enhance their time management skills and incorporate new techniques, there's a fundamental step that is often overlooked: self-assessment. This means pausing, stepping back, and critically evaluating one's existing time management habits. Here's a guide to conducting this introspection:

1. The Need for Reflection:

The first step is acknowledging the necessity of this reflection. Without a clear picture of current habits, integrating new techniques becomes like shooting arrows in the dark. By understanding how you currently allocate time, you can tailor time management strategies to fit your unique needs and challenges.

2. Task Logging:

Imagine trying to diagnose an issue with a machine without understanding its operations. Similarly, to identify time management challenges, one needs to track daily activities. For a week, maintain a detailed log. Every task, no matter how trivial, from work-related activities to leisurely coffee breaks, should be noted. In today's digital age, manual logging can be supplemented or even replaced by tools. Applications like Toggl or RescueTime automatically track digital activities, providing a clear breakdown of how much time is spent on various applications and websites.

3. Identify Time-Wasters:

Once the week concludes, it's time for the revelation. Review the logs and pinpoint areas where time seems to dissipate. For some, it might be the seemingly innocuous checks on social media that cumulatively add up to hours. For others, it could be frequent breaks that, instead of being rejuvenating pauses, become prolonged periods of inactivity. Maybe there are redundant tasks in your work process, or perhaps meetings that could have been emails. The key here is to be honest and ruthless in this evaluation. Remember, identifying a problem is the first step to solving it.

4. Creating a Baseline:

This assessment is not meant to be an exercise in self-criticism. Instead, it provides a baseline. It's a snapshot of your current time management habits. By understanding where you stand, you can set clear, measurable goals for improvement. Moreover, revisiting this assessment after integrating new techniques can provide tangible evidence of progress, serving as a motivational boost.

Time, as they say, waits for no one. However, how we choose to spend it remains in our hands. By taking the time to understand our existing habits, we empower ourselves with the knowledge to make meaningful changes. This initial assessment, though seemingly simple, lays the foundation for a structured and effective approach to time management. Armed with these insights, one is better equipped to navigate the myriad techniques and strategies of time management, ensuring they are not just applied but optimized for individual needs.

Setting Clear Objectives:

At the heart of every pursuit, be it personal or professional, lies a set of objectives. Time, as a resource, is finite. How we channel it towards our ambitions determines our trajectory towards these objectives. In the realm of time management, setting clear goals is not just recommended; it's imperative. Let's delve into the significance of objectives and how they shape our time management endeavors.

1. The North Star:

Objectives serve as our guiding star, a beacon that lends direction amidst the chaos of daily tasks and responsibilities. Think about a ship in the vast ocean; without a clear destination, it drifts aimlessly. Similarly, without clear objectives, our daily efforts can become disjointed and reactive rather than proactive. Whether it's an aspiration to rise through the ranks in a corporate setting, the dream of launching a groundbreaking startup, the passion to pen a best-selling novel, or the simple yet profound goal of striking a harmonious work-life balance, these objectives shape our daily actions.

2. Macro vs. Micro:

Objectives can broadly be divided into two categories: long-term (macro) and short-term (micro). Long-term goals might include career milestones or life ambitions that might take years to achieve. On the other hand, short-term goals are more immediate, possibly achievable within weeks or months. For instance, while launching a successful startup might be a long-term objective, securing the first round of funding or developing the prototype could be short-term goals. Both are crucial. The macro goals provide the vision, while the micro goals lay out the roadmap to achieve that vision.

3. Time Allocation Aligned with Objectives:

Once objectives are delineated, they play a pivotal role in time allocation. Activities that align with our objectives should command priority. For example, if your goal is to write a novel, then dedicated writing blocks should feature prominently in your daily or weekly schedule. If climbing the corporate ladder is the ambition, then tasks that enhance skills, visibility, and contribute directly to company goals become paramount.

4. Periodic Review and Refinement:

Setting objectives is not a one-time activity. As we evolve, so do our goals. It's essential to periodically review and, if necessary, refine these objectives. This ensures that our time management strategies remain relevant and effective. A goal set two years ago might have been achieved or might no longer align with current aspirations. Regularly revisiting objectives ensures that our efforts are always channeled in the right direction.

Objectives are the foundation upon which effective time management stands. They infuse our days with purpose, ensuring that every hour spent is a step towards a cherished goal. In the intricate dance of tasks, breaks, priorities, and downtimes, clear objectives are the rhythm that ensures we move with purpose and intent. By identifying, prioritizing, and regularly reviewing these objectives, we ensure that our time management strategies are not just about doing more, but more importantly, about doing what truly matters.

Prioritizing Tasks:

In our daily hustle, every task often screams for immediate attention. However, all tasks are not created equal. Distinguishing between what is crucial and what can wait is at the heart of successful time management. This pivotal skill of prioritization allows us to channel our energies effectively. Here's a comprehensive exploration of strategies that can aid in aligning tasks with goals.

Understanding Relative Values:

To craft a meaningful day, it's pivotal to discern the relative importance of tasks. Which endeavors directly align with your broader goals? Which ones have immediate consequences? Evaluating tasks based on their significance and urgency creates a hierarchy, serving as a beacon for your daily activities.

Identifying the Big Rocks:

Think of your day as a container, with tasks being the rocks, pebbles, and sand you fill it with. The 'big rocks' represent your primary, non-negotiable tasks. If you start by addressing minor tasks (the sand), there may not be room left for these essential activities. Addressing these high-impact tasks first ensures they aren't sidelined.

Utilizing the Eisenhower Box:

The Eisenhower Box (or matrix) is a powerful visualization tool that divides tasks into four quadrants based on their urgency and importance. This categorization helps in determining which tasks need immediate attention, which ones can be scheduled for later, which can be delegated, and which can be eliminated from your list.

Employing the 4 D's to Refine Your List:

After broadly categorizing tasks using the Eisenhower Box, delve deeper using the 4 D's framework:

- **Delete:** Identify and remove tasks that don't contribute meaningfully to your objectives.

- **Delegate:** Recognize tasks that others might be better equipped to handle. Efficient delegation ensures the right fit between a task and its executor.

- **Defer:** Some tasks, while valuable, might not be pressing. Assign them to a future slot when they can be adequately addressed.

- **Do:** Tasks that demand immediate attention fall into this category. With a streamlined list, addressing these becomes more manageable.

Harnessing the Pareto Principle:

The 80/20 rule, derived from Vilfredo Pareto's observations, indicates that a select few tasks (approximately 20%) will deliver the bulk of your results (around 80%). Identifying and focusing on these high-impact tasks can maximize your outcomes and ensure optimal use of time.

Prioritizing tasks isn't merely about listing them but about aligning them strategically with desired outcomes. With tools like the Eisenhower Box and the Pareto Principle, combined with techniques like the 4 D's, task management transforms from a mere daily chore to a strategic endeavor. By carefully sifting through tasks, understanding their significance, and allocating energies accordingly, one ensures not only productivity but also the satisfaction of time well-spent. Such an approach guarantees that efforts are laser-focused on what truly matters, ensuring a sense of purpose and progress in every day.

Structuring Time

In the intricate dance of daily responsibilities, having clear priorities is only half the battle won. The other half revolves around effectively structuring your time to honor these priorities. With a myriad of tasks vying for attention, carving out a thoughtful structure for the day can significantly enhance productivity and mental clarity. Here's a deep dive into two potent techniques to architect a day that resonates with purpose and efficiency.

1. Time Boxing:

At its essence, time boxing is about setting clear boundaries. Instead of letting tasks sprawl unchecked, this technique involves allocating specific blocks of time to each task. The beauty of time boxing lies in its visual nature. By translating tasks into tangible blocks on a calendar, one gains a bird's eye view of the day, facilitating informed decisions about task sequencing and duration.

- **Buffer Times:** While it's tempting to pack tasks back-to-back, the inclusion of buffer times is crucial. These are short, intentional breaks that allow the mind to reset, especially when transitioning between tasks of diverse natures. For instance, after an intense brainstorming session, a buffer time could be the breather you need before diving into administrative tasks. It's this ebb and flow, this rhythmic alternation between focused work and relaxation, that sustains productivity without leading to burnout.

- **Calendar Commitment:** Time boxes achieve their true potential when they are integrated into one's calendar. Whether it's a digital calendar or a physical planner, visualizing these time blocks reinforces commitment, serving as a reminder of the day's blueprint.

2. Pomodoro Technique:

Crafted by Francesco Cirillo, the Pomodoro Technique is a testament to the power of focused bursts of activity. By breaking tasks into intervals (traditionally 25 minutes) followed by short breaks, this method champions the idea that concentration is best maintained in sprints rather than marathons.

- **Customization:** While 25 minutes is the widely recognized standard, the true spirit of the Pomodoro Technique lies in its flexibility. If a task demands a rhythm that doesn't quite align with this timeframe, feel free to adjust. Perhaps your sweet spot is 40 minutes of work followed by a 10-minute break. The key is to find a rhythm that aligns with the task at hand and your personal work style.

Structuring time is akin to sculpting: it's the art of chiseling away the superfluous to reveal the masterpiece within. Techniques like Time Boxing and the Pomodoro serve as the sculptor's tools, facilitating the creation of a day that not only brims with productivity but also resonates with intention and purpose. By committing to these structures, one ensures that each moment is spent in alignment with one's priorities, ensuring a harmonious blend of achievement and satisfaction.

Calendar Management:

In today's bustling world, managing time effectively has become paramount. A robust calendar, meticulously maintained, acts as the fulcrum, balancing our personal and professional endeavors. It's more than a mere date tracker; it's our daily blueprint, a tangible reflection of our priorities, commitments, and aspirations.

1. Include Everything:

For a calendar to truly serve its purpose, it must paint a comprehensive picture of our day. This means everything, from the significant business presentation to the 10-minute coffee break, must find its place. Appointments, tasks, breaks, leisure activities, personal errands, and more should be recorded. For example, if you're committing to a new fitness regimen, block that early morning hour for your workout. This not only ensures adherence but also helps you plan around it.

2. Block Off Time for Tasks:

While meetings and appointments often naturally find their way onto calendars, tasks might be overlooked. It's crucial to allocate specific blocks of time for individual tasks. This practice, known as time boxing, helps ensure that tasks don't remain endless endeavors but have defined start and finish times. It fosters a sense of commitment to completing the task within the designated window. For instance, if you've been struggling to make headway on a report, block out a two-hour window exclusively for that. During this period, the report isn't just something you *could* work on; it's what you're committed to working on.

3. Daily and Weekly Reviews:

A calendar shouldn't be static. Its true potential is realized through dynamic interaction. A morning review primes the mind, setting the stage for the day's performance. It acts as a daily touchpoint, ensuring alignment with the day's objectives. On the other hand, the weekly review is more strategic. It's the opportunity to assess the week gone by, plan for the upcoming one, adjust for any changes, and ensure a balance between various commitments.

Perhaps you noticed during your review that personal reading time has been consistently missed; now's your chance to block time for it in the coming week.

4. Flexibility:

Rigidity in a calendar can be a recipe for stress. Life is peppered with unpredictability. While the calendar provides structure, it should also accommodate the unexpected. Whether it's the unscheduled call that runs long or an unforeseen task that crops up, the calendar should be adaptable. Building in buffer times, keeping some slots intentionally open, or being mentally ready to adjust ensures that the calendar remains an organizational aid, not a straitjacket.

5. Embrace Adaptability:

The essence of an effective calendar doesn't lie in its rigidity but its adaptability. While a structured approach is vital, life's unpredictability necessitates flexibility. A last-minute meeting, an unexpected visitor, or an unplanned task can disrupt a tightly-packed calendar. Instead of perceiving the calendar as an unyielding framework, view it as a dynamic guide. By incorporating buffer times, leaving some slots unoccupied, or being mentally prepared to reshuffle, we ensure our calendar remains an organizational asset, not a stressor.

In the modern maze of endless tasks and commitments, an adeptly managed calendar stands as a beacon, guiding us to effective time management. It becomes our daily script, ensuring each day unfolds with clarity, purpose, and adaptability, all while staying aligned with our broader objectives.

Embracing Tools and Technology:

The digital era has blessed us with a plethora of tools and applications designed to augment our time management abilities. By integrating these technological marvels into our daily routines, we can not only optimize our productivity but also infuse a layer of efficiency and organization into our schedules.

1. Task Managers:

In the whirlwind of daily commitments, it's all too easy for tasks to become lost or overlooked. Enter task managers– digital saviors that help us collate, categorize, and conquer our to-dos. Apps like **Todoist** offer intuitive interfaces, allowing users to quickly jot down tasks, set deadlines, and even prioritize them. With features like recurring tasks and project categorization, Todoist ensures no task falls through the cracks. On the other hand, **Trello** adopts a board-based approach, reminiscent of a digital Kanban board. Here, tasks are represented as cards, which can be shuffled between columns representing different stages of completion. Whether you're tracking a complex project or just managing daily chores, these tools offer visual and structured avenues to stay on top of tasks.

2. Digital Calendars:

Gone are the days of manual, paper-based calendars. Modern digital calendars, like **Google Calendar** or **Microsoft Outlook**, offer multifaceted functionalities that go beyond mere date tracking. For one, the ability to set and receive reminders ensures that you're always primed for upcoming commitments. Need to prepare for a big presentation? Set a reminder a day before to revise. Additionally, the ability to color-code appointments, integrate with other apps, and access your calendar across devices amplifies its utility. Whether it's a doctor's appointment, a team meeting, or a lunch date, the digital calendar stands as your personal assistant, ensuring you're always in the right place at the right time.

3. Pomodoro Apps:

The Pomodoro Technique, with its structured work-break cycles, has garnered accolades for boosting productivity and focus.

However, continually monitoring a timer can be distracting. This is where Pomodoro apps come into play. These tools, tailored specifically for the technique, automate the timing process. They ring alarms at the end of work intervals, initiate break timers, and even track the number of Pomodoros completed. With apps like this, you're free to immerse yourself in the task at hand, assured that the app will notify you when it's time to pause or resume.

Time, often touted as our most valuable resource, warrants management with precision and foresight. In this pursuit, modern tools and technology serve as invaluable allies. They encapsulate best practices, automate routine processes, and present data-driven insights, ensuring that our journey towards optimal time management is both effective and efficient. By embracing these digital companions, we position ourselves for success in an increasingly fast-paced world.

Execution: The Heartbeat of Time Management

While planning and strategizing are the backbone of effective time management, execution is its lifeblood. The most meticulous plans hold little value unless translated into actionable steps. Execution is where ideas meet reality, strategies bear fruit, and progress is achieved.

1. Completing Tasks on the To-Do List:

The satisfaction of checking off a task from a to-do list is unmatched. It's a tangible indicator of progress and achievement. However, this requires discipline. It's essential to resist the urge to jump to newer tasks before completing the ones at hand. As you cross out completed tasks, it not only provides a sense of accomplishment but also offers clarity on what lies ahead.

2. Meeting Deadlines:

Deadlines are the lifelines of productivity. They instill a sense of purpose and urgency. Ensuring you meet or even better, beat deadlines, showcases professionalism, reliability, and commitment. It's about respecting not just your time, but others' as well. Utilize reminders, alarms, and even peer accountability to stay on track.

3. Punctuality for Meetings:

Being punctual is a non-verbal signal of respect. It conveys your regard for others' time and demonstrates professionalism. Always factor in buffer time, especially if commuting, to ensure you're never late.

4. Note-Taking and Organization:

As you engage in meetings, discussions, or even personal reflections, taking notes is crucial. It's a way to capture insights, action points, and ideas. But, raw notes can often seem chaotic. Post-meeting, invest time to organize these notes, categorize them, and highlight actionable items. Tools like Evernote or Notion can be invaluable allies in this endeavor.

5. Rescheduling Meetings:

Life is unpredictable. Sometimes, despite our best efforts, we might need to reschedule meetings. In such cases, it's pivotal to communicate promptly and propose alternative slots. It's also beneficial to understand the reason behind the rescheduling—if it's a recurring factor, addressing it might improve overall time management.

6. Keeping Track:

With a multitude of tasks, commitments, and responsibilities, maintaining a tracking system is indispensable. Whether it's a physical planner, a digital tool, or a combination of both, find what resonates with you. Regularly update it, and at intervals, review it to ensure you're aligned with your goals.

Execution is the bridge between intent and reality. While the tools, techniques, and strategies form the blueprint, it's in the realm of execution that the edifice of productivity is built. It requires a blend of discipline, adaptability, and foresight. By mastering the art of execution, you ensure that your time management efforts yield tangible, meaningful results, propelling you closer to your goals with each passing day.

Continuous Reflection and Adjustment:

Time management, akin to many other skills and practices in our lives, is not static. It's an ever-evolving discipline, influenced by changes in our personal lives, professional scenarios, and even broader world events. Recognizing this dynamic nature is crucial for anyone serious about maximizing their productivity and achieving their goals.

1. The Power of Monthly Reviews:

The idea of setting aside a specific day each month for a review can be transformative. This is not just an audit of tasks accomplished but a holistic overview of how your time management practices are impacting your broader life objectives. Did you find yourself perpetually rushed, even though you met all your deadlines? Were there tasks that consumed disproportionate amounts of time with little to no tangible outputs? Asking such questions can help pinpoint inefficiencies and areas of improvement.

For instance, you might realize that while you've been timely with your project submissions, the incessant multitasking has left you feeling drained, leading to reduced quality in your deliverables. Or perhaps, you note that while you've been punctual with your professional commitments, your personal life or self-care routines have taken a hit.

2. Embracing Change and Adaptability:

An essential facet of these reviews is the willingness to change. Time management techniques are tools. If a tool isn't delivering the desired results, it's prudent to re-evaluate its relevance. For some, the Pomodoro Technique with its structured intervals might seem stifling. They might find that slightly longer work intervals with extended breaks align better with their work rhythm.

Similarly, life doesn't operate in silos. A sudden personal commitment or an unexpected project at work can demand a significant shift in how you manage your time. Being rigid and holding onto a previously set routine might lead to inefficiencies or burnout. Instead, adaptability, the ability to tweak, adjust, or even overhaul your time management strategies, ensures that you remain effective irrespective of changing circumstances.

Moreover, the world of time management is vast, with myriad techniques and tools. If one doesn't resonate, there's always another to experiment with. This iterative process of trial, review, and adjustment ensures that your time management practices remain aligned with your evolving goals and life situations.

Time management, at its heart, is a deeply personal endeavor. It's a reflection of one's values, objectives, and priorities. As these shift and evolve, so must the techniques employed to manage time. Continuous reflection, coupled with a readiness to adapt, ensures that your relationship with time remains productive, fulfilling, and in harmony with your overarching life vision.

Balancing Rigor with Relaxation:

In the relentless pursuit of productivity, it's easy to fall into the trap of seeing every minute as a potential slot for work, every hour as an opportunity to tick off another task from the to-do list. The allure of a jam-packed calendar, filled with back-to-back tasks and commitments, might seem like the epitome of efficiency. However, true time management transcends mere task completion. It delves deeper, striking a harmonious balance between rigorous work and meaningful relaxation.

1. The Value of Downtime:

Our society often glorifies the "hustle culture," where relentless work is celebrated as a badge of honor. But this constant grind can be counterproductive. Our brains are not wired to be in a perpetual state of exertion. Just as muscles need rest after intense exercise, our minds too require downtime after concentrated periods of work. This isn't just about preventing burnout; it's about enhancing overall productivity. Numerous studies highlight that breaks can boost creativity, improve concentration, and enhance problem-solving skills. It's in these moments of rest that our brains process information, form connections, and often come up with the most innovative ideas.

2. Scheduled Relaxation vs. Spontaneous Breaks:

While the Pomodoro Technique emphasizes structured breaks after set intervals, there's also merit in spontaneous relaxation. Maybe it's stepping out for an impromptu walk on a sunny day, taking a few minutes to meditate when stressed, or simply indulging in a midday nap when fatigue sets in. These unscheduled breaks, driven by intuition and self-awareness, can be just as rejuvenating as planned ones.

3. Beyond Productivity: The Mental Health Perspective:

An essential, often overlooked facet of time management is its impact on mental well-being. A schedule devoid of relaxation can lead to heightened stress, anxiety, and even burnout. Ensuring pockets of relaxation, be it through hobbies, spending time with loved ones, or simply indulging in moments of stillness, is paramount for emotional equilibrium.

4. The Bigger Picture:

Time management, in its essence, is a tool for life optimization. It's not just about maximizing work output but enhancing the quality of life. Relaxation, in this framework, isn't an optional extra but an integral component. It's these moments of pause that give meaning to the hustle, offering clarity, perspective, and a renewed zest for the tasks ahead.

Balancing rigor with relaxation is not a luxury; it's a necessity. It's the dance between doing and being, between exertion and rest, that crafts a life of purpose, productivity, and peace. As we sculpt our schedules, ensuring space for both endeavors not only optimizes our output but enriches our overall life experience.

Conclusion:

Building a holistic time management routine is akin to constructing a personalized machine, where each gear and lever represents a different technique or principle. When they work in tandem, the machine operates smoothly, driving you towards your goals. By continually assessing, reflecting, and adjusting, you ensure that your time management machinery remains well-oiled and effective, propelling you towards both personal and professional success.

PART II

TACTICS FOR EFFICIENT TIME MANAGEMENT

The journey towards mastering time is paved with various strategies and insights. In this section, "Tactics for Efficient Time Management," we delve into specific, actionable tactics that can drastically enhance how we approach, utilize, and value our time. These chapters collectively provide a roadmap to navigating the complexities of daily routines, deadlines, and tasks, ensuring that time is always on our side.

Chapter 9: Busily Waiting:

The concept of "busily waiting" redefines downtime. It prompts us to capitalize on moments that might traditionally be overlooked or underutilized. This chapter elaborates on the significance of this tactic in today's dynamic environment, offering practical examples and guiding readers on incorporating 'busily waiting' seamlessly into their daily lives.

Chapter 10: Thoughtless Productivity:

Multitasking has often been both praised and vilified. However, "Thoughtless Productivity" takes a fresh perspective on this, illustrating how one can combine tasks to foster efficiency without cognitive drain. The science of multitasking is dissected, and the chapter offers strategies that empower individuals to pair activities effectively, maximizing outcomes.

Chapter 11: Front-end Loading:

Diving into the realms of Parkinson's Law and the Student Syndrome, this chapter champions the tactic of front-end loading. Readers will understand the profound impact of tackling significant segments of tasks upfront and will be provided with a structured approach to adopt this method, reaping its manifold benefits.

Chapter 12: Early Deadlines:

Deadlines, when used effectively, can be potent motivational tools. This chapter delves deep into the psychology of deadlines and advocates for the proactive setting of earlier, self-imposed timeframes. By exploring the advantages of this approach and offering guidance on its implementation, readers will learn to harness the power of deadlines as productivity catalysts.

Chapter 13: Buffer Management:

The unpredictable nature of life necessitates a strategy that accounts for uncertainties: buffer management. Emphasizing the importance of building in safety nets within plans, this chapter arms readers with techniques to create and leverage buffers. This ensures that unexpected challenges are met with preparedness and flexibility.

These five techniques yield small improvements. However, when used consistently and in concert with each other, these have a compounding effect and help you become much more efficient and productive.

CHAPTER 9

Busily Waiting

Definition and Relevance

Waiting has become an inherent part of our daily routines. Whether it's the minutes ticking away at the doctor's office or the brief pause at a traffic signal, these pockets of time often go unnoticed and unutilized. "Busily Waiting" is a structured approach to harness these seemingly inconsequential moments, transforming them into productive intervals.

Johnny Carson humorously quipped about the shortest interval of time being the gap between a Manhattan traffic light turning green and the honk of an impatient cab driver. This aptly encapsulates our collective impatience. But more than just an observation about our intolerance to delays, it underscores a broader truth: many of us simply don't know how to wait.

People who often express the most frustration about waiting, be it for inefficient sales clerks or bank tellers, are usually those least equipped to manage this idle time. In contrast, others swiftly whip out their devices, delving into games, conversations, or videos, creating their own bubble of engagement.

But what if, instead of mere distractions, we could turn these waits into genuinely productive intervals?

The philosophy of "Busily Waiting" suggests just that. By identifying potential waiting scenarios in advance and equipping ourselves with tasks that can be tackled during these gaps, we can significantly enhance our productivity.

Examples of Situations Where This Tactic is Applicable

Imagine you're at a doctor's clinic. The receptionist informs you of an unexpected delay, resulting in an additional 20-minute wait. For many, this would be a source of annoyance. However, with the "Busily Waiting" approach, this time can be transformed. Perhaps you use these moments to draft and send out a few pending emails, or maybe you delve into a chapter of a book you've been meaning to read.

Another common scenario: you're at the grocery store. The lines are longer than usual. Instead of fidgeting or aimlessly browsing through social media, you could utilize this time to mentally plan your week ahead, list down any additional items you might need, or even engage in a mindfulness exercise to rejuvenate your mind.

Then there's public transport. Whether it's a daily commute or a sporadic journey, buses, trains, and flights often come with waits. This could be the perfect time to listen to an informative podcast, brush up on industry news, or even indulge in a short meditation session.

The examples are endless. The beauty of "Busily Waiting" lies in its versatility. Whether you're awaiting a meeting to start, sitting in a café for a friend who's running late, or just standing in line at the post office, these pockets of time are everywhere, waiting to be harnessed.

Rules for Busily Waiting:

1. Portability

Definition: The core of portability revolves around the ability of a task to be easily carried out irrespective of where you are, primarily utilizing compact tools or devices.

Scenarios:

Compact Physical Tools: Tasks that require pocket-sized tools, like jotting down ideas in a small notebook.

Digital Portability: Activities that can be carried out on smartphones or tablets, like managing emails, reading articles, or listening to podcasts.

Mental Tasks: Activities like brainstorming, where the primary tool is one's own thoughts.

Examples: Imagine you're waiting in a long line at the bank. Whipping out a laptop to draft a presentation would be impractical. However, a task like sketching out a mind map of the presentation's flow on a pocket notebook or mentally conceptualizing the presentation's key points would be apt.

2.   Location Independence

Definition: A task's ability to be executed without being bound to a specific venue or set of resources.

Scenarios:

No Specific Tools Required: Tasks that don't rely on particular tools exclusive to a location, like certain office equipment.

Digital Cloud Accessibility: Jobs that can be tackled anywhere thanks to cloud storage, allowing access to files from various devices.

Mental Independence: Tasks that solely rely on cognitive processes, devoid of any external aids.

Examples: Consider having to review a document. If the document is stored only on your office desktop, it becomes location-dependent. Conversely, if it's saved on a cloud service, you can review it on a mobile device during a metro ride, epitomizing location independence.

3. Task Nature

Definition: This rule emphasizes matching the inherent characteristics of a task with the nature and expected duration of the wait.

Scenarios:

Short-burst Tasks: Tasks that can be executed quickly and don't require a long, continuous time frame, like replying to a text or making a quick checklist.

Segmentable Tasks: Larger tasks that can be broken down into smaller chunks. Each chunk can fit different waiting durations, allowing for parts of a bigger task to be completed across multiple waits.

Continuous Tasks: Tasks that, once initiated, should ideally not be broken up, like deep reading or tasks that require extended concentration.

Examples: If you're waiting for your coffee to be made at a cafe, a short-burst task like sending a quick email would be fitting. On the other hand, if you're at a salon expecting a prolonged wait, segmentable tasks, like planning out a week's schedule or reading a few chapters of a book, would be more appropriate. In contrast, if a task demands sustained attention, it might be best reserved for more predictable, uninterrupted spans, like dedicated work hours, or while waiting for your car to have an oil change or regular service (a half-hour or so).

Steps to Implement Busily Waiting in Daily Life

1. Plan and Anticipate

Explanation: Proactive anticipation is the foundation of the "Busily Waiting" approach. By foreseeing potential waiting situations, you can harness otherwise wasted moments for productivity.

Example: Imagine you have a doctor's appointment. While the appointment itself might be fixed, the time spent in the waiting room can be unpredictable. Recognizing this in advance allows you to prepare a task to complete during that time, transforming idle moments into productive ones.

2. Categorize Your Tasks

Explanation: Categorization provides clarity, ensuring that you match tasks with appropriate waiting scenarios. Distinguishing tasks based on their nature, location-dependency, and time requirement is crucial.

Example: If you're creating a to-do list and one item is "Draft Monthly Report," you might label it as non-portable, location-specific (as it needs resources from the office), and requiring a block of dedicated time. Conversely, "Read Industry News" might be portable, location-independent, and chunkable. I use symbols such as an anchor for location-specific (not movable) tasks, a solid block for dedicated time tasks, a feather for a portable lightweight task, and a slice of pizza for a portable chunkable (slice = chunk, get it?) task. You could use symbols or letters, e.g., "L" for location-specific, "B" for solid block, etc.

3. Equip Yourself

Explanation: Being armed with the right tools ensures you can effectively dive into tasks during waiting times.

Example: If you're heading to a cafe and expect a short wait, having a small notebook in your bag allows you to quickly sketch out ideas. Similarly, if you've planned to learn from online tutorials during a long commute, having your headphones ensures you can watch without disruptions.

4. Match Tasks with Waits

Explanation: Effective "Busily Waiting" isn't about tackling any task during waits, but about aligning the right task with the waiting duration and environment.

Example: At a bus stop where you expect a ten-minute wait, you might choose to clear out junk emails. But during a 30-minute subway ride, you might decide to dive into a podcast episode about industry trends.

5. Stay Flexible

Explanation: "Busily Waiting" isn't rigid. It requires adaptability, ensuring that you can adjust to the unpredictable nature of waiting times without getting frustrated.

Example: Suppose you've reserved a long article to read during a train journey, but there's an unexpected delay. Instead of getting agitated, you switch to another task, like brainstorming ideas for an upcoming presentation, ensuring continued productivity.

6. Review and Adjust

Explanation: Reflection is vital to refine your approach. By regularly evaluating your "Busily Waiting" experiences, you can continually optimize your strategy for future waits.

Example: After a week, you realize that the articles you saved for reading during short breaks weren't as engaging in those settings. On reflection, you decide to switch to listening to short podcast snippets during such breaks, aligning better with the waiting environment.

Remember, the essence of "Busily Waiting" isn't just about relentless productivity. It's about recognizing and utilizing pockets of time that would otherwise slip away unnoticed. By judiciously employing these moments, not only do we achieve more, but we also alleviate the frustration that often accompanies waits, making our days more fulfilling and efficient.

CHAPTER 10

Thoughtless Productivity

Introduction to Thoughtless Productivity

Definition

"Thoughtless Productivity" might seem like an oxymoron at first glance. Productivity often conjures images of intense focus, detailed planning, and dedicated effort. So, how can it be 'thoughtless'? But, this term doesn't denote a lack of thought or carelessness. Instead, it encapsulates the idea of achieving productivity almost effortlessly, without the constant need for intense cognitive engagement.

In essence, "Thoughtless Productivity" refers to the ability to be productive in tasks without investing a significant amount of conscious thought or deliberation. It's about automating certain actions or tasks to such a degree that they become second nature, similar to how one might drive a familiar route without actively thinking about each turn.

The implications of this concept are vast. Firstly, it underscores the potential to free up cognitive bandwidth. When certain tasks become routine or automated, our minds are liberated to focus on more demanding, novel, or creative endeavors. Secondly, it speaks to the importance of habit formation in productivity. Just as a musician might practice scales until they can play them without thinking, similarly, repetitive practice or exposure to certain tasks can lead to them becoming 'thoughtlessly' productive.

In a world where cognitive overload is a real concern, the ability to offload some tasks to the realm of 'thoughtless' execution can be a game-changer. It's not about mindlessness, but rather about harnessing the power of habit, routine, and familiarity to enhance efficiency and efficacy in our daily endeavors.

Importance

In our rapidly evolving world, brimming with endless tasks and constant stimuli, efficient time management is more than just a skill—it's a survival tool. Amidst this chaos, thoughtless productivity emerges as a beacon of efficiency, presenting a method to manage time effectively and achieve more with less conscious effort.

Thoughtless productivity is not about doing things without care but about transitioning repeated tasks into autopilot mode. Think of the countless decisions and actions we make daily. If every decision required intense deliberation, we'd be exhausted by noon! By automating certain tasks, we free up mental bandwidth, making room for innovation, creativity, and more complex problem-solving.

Moreover, in a productivity landscape where multi-tasking is often misinterpreted as efficiency, thoughtless productivity offers a genuine solution. Instead of juggling tasks with divided attention, it enables us to execute routine tasks seamlessly, almost as background processes, while our conscious mind focuses on novel challenges.

Furthermore, the reduced cognitive load decreases the risk of burnout. Constant decision-making and task-switching can be mentally taxing. However, when tasks transition to the realm of 'thoughtless', they demand less mental energy, paving the way for sustainable productivity.

In conclusion, thoughtless productivity isn't about mindless action; it's strategic efficiency. In harnessing it, we not only optimize our time but also protect our most valuable resource: our cognitive energy. By achieving more with less conscious effort, it truly stands as a game-changer in our quest for productivity and balance.

Unraveling the Myths of Multi-tasking

Definition of Multi-tasking

Multi-tasking, as the term suggests, refers to the simultaneous execution of more than one task. At its core, multi-tasking involves switching attention between tasks rapidly, giving the illusion of doing them concurrently. In today's digital age, this concept has become synonymous with efficiency and time optimization. A typical example includes checking emails while participating in a conference call or scrolling through social media while watching television.

However, a crucial distinction exists between true simultaneous tasking (like walking while talking) and rapid task-switching (like writing a report and frequently shifting to emails). While the former can be achieved without significant cognitive interference, the latter often disrupts focus and diminishes the quality of output for both tasks.

In essence, multi-tasking is a double-edged sword. While it might seem like a route to increased productivity, it often leads to decreased attention spans, higher error rates, and longer task completion times. Understanding its true nature helps individuals harness its potential benefits while being wary of its pitfalls.

The Brain and Multi-tasking: A Neuroscientific Perspective

In the mid-20th century, cognitive psychologist George A. Miller posited that the average number of objects an individual can hold in their working memory is about seven. This "magical number," 7 +/- 2, has since been widely cited in psychology. However, while our brains might be able to store multiple items in short-term memory, the actual focus of our cognitive resources on tasks is singular in nature.

From a neurological perspective, multi-tasking doesn't mean the brain is processing tasks simultaneously, as computers might with parallel processing. Instead, it rapidly toggles between tasks, which takes place in the prefrontal cortex, the brain's control center. This switch might seem instantaneous, but it requires a series of intricate neurocognitive processes.

When we attempt to perform multiple tasks that require cognitive attention, our brain has to decide which task to prioritize. This decision-making process consumes valuable time and cognitive resources. The brain must then disengage from one task, move to the next, re-orient itself, and then engage with this new task. These continual shifts can introduce cognitive lag, making multi-tasking inefficient.

Furthermore, as we force our brains into this relentless toggling, we run the risk of depleting neurotransmitters essential for focus and attention. The result? Decreased productivity, increased susceptibility to errors, and mental fatigue.

It's also worth noting the effects of external interruptions on this already complex process. Modern life is rife with distractions, from smartphone notifications to sudden background noises. When juggling tasks, our brain becomes even more receptive to these disruptions, leading to further diffused attention.

However, a nuance to this understanding is the concept of pre-emptive multitasking. While true simultaneous cognitive multitasking is challenging, our brains are capable of conscious pre-emptive multitasking. This means focusing intently on one thought at a time, but swiftly switching between thoughts. A classic example of this ability can be observed in chess grandmasters who can simultaneously play blindfolded chess against multiple opponents. They don't track every game at once. Instead, they rapidly switch their focus from one board to another, recalling and analyzing each game's unique position. Achieving this level of concentration, however, demands rigorous practice and an ability to maintain an elevated level of concentration. Remarkably, with enough training, the human brain can sustain such intense efforts for extended periods without excessive mental wear.

In conclusion, while our innate neural architecture might lean towards deep, singular focus, with training and practice, we can harness the power of rapid, sequential attention. This blend of understanding our cognitive limits and pushing our boundaries can lead to optimized productivity and mental prowess.

Multi-tasking: Weighing the Pros and Cons

■ Pros of Multi-tasking:

1. **Increased Productivity in Routine Tasks:** Multi-tasking can be beneficial when performing tasks that don't demand high cognitive attention. For instance, listening to a podcast or an audiobook while doing household chores or exercise allows you to consume information without detracting from the primary activity. In such scenarios, you can effectively accomplish two tasks simultaneously without compromising the quality of either.

2. **Enhanced Adaptability:** In today's fast-paced digital environment, there's often a demand to juggle multiple inputs,

especially in roles like customer support or reception duties. Being able to handle multiple tasks or inputs in rapid succession can make an individual more adaptable and agile in roles that demand such skills. Over time, this can train the brain to switch between tasks more quickly, improving response times.

3. **Better Time Utilization:** Multi-tasking can, in certain contexts, make the most of limited time. If you're on a tight schedule, replying to emails while waiting in a queue or brainstorming ideas during a long commute can help utilize what might otherwise be 'dead' time.

■ Cons of Multi-tasking:

1. **Compromised Quality:** When you split your attention between tasks that require cognitive effort, the quality of work often suffers. The brain's constant toggling between tasks can lead to more errors, lack of depth in understanding, and superficial completion. For instance, reading an important document while continually checking social media will likely result in missed details or a lack of comprehensive understanding.

2. **Reduced Efficiency:** Contrary to popular belief, multi-tasking doesn't always save time. In fact, it often takes more total time to complete tasks when you jump between them than if you

finish them sequentially. This is due to the cognitive costs of task-switching, where the brain needs time to adjust each time you shift focus.

3. **Increased Stress and Mental Fatigue:** Multi-tasking can be mentally exhausting. The constant need to reorient oneself with each task switch can lead to faster cognitive drain, reducing the total productive time available. Moreover, when tasks aren't completed efficiently or to a satisfactory standard due to divided attention, it can lead to feelings of stress or inadequacy.

4. **Impaired Memory and Learning:** Studies have shown that multi-tasking, especially when it involves media or technology, can impair the brain's ability to both form and retrieve memories. For example, students who browse the internet or check their phones while attending a lecture or studying typically retain less information than those who focus solely on the learning task.

In conclusion, while multi-tasking might offer some advantages in specific contexts, it's essential to be discerning about its application. Recognizing when to multi-task and when to dedicate focused attention can be the key to effective and efficient work.

The Efficiency of Task Combination

Time management isn't just about organizing tasks; it's also about knowing when to combine them for maximum efficiency. By judiciously pairing tasks, we can often get more done in less time. However, the efficiency of task combination largely depends on the nature of the tasks being paired. Here's a closer look:

1. **Task Compatibility:** Task compatibility refers to the ability to perform two or more tasks simultaneously without compromising the quality or efficiency of either. At the core of this is the cognitive load that each task demands. If one task requires significant cognitive processing and the other is more automatic or habitual, they might be compatible. On the contrary, if both tasks demand high attention, combining them might lead to errors, decreased efficiency, and increased cognitive fatigue.

   For instance, attempting to read a detailed report while actively participating in a meeting would be incompatible. Both tasks require significant cognitive resources, making it unlikely that either would be done well. On the other hand, walking (a largely automatic task) while discussing a project over the phone (a cognitive task) might be compatible for many.

2. **Effective Pairings:** Certain tasks naturally complement each other, creating synergies when combined. For example:

- **Listening and Physical Tasks:** As previously mentioned, listening to a podcast, audiobook, or music can pair well with household chores, exercising, or commuting. The reason is that the cognitive load of listening does not interfere with the motor skills required for these physical tasks.

- **Waiting and Quick Tasks:** If you're waiting in line or for an appointment, it can be an excellent time to check and respond to emails, plan your day, or even catch up on some light reading.

- **Watching and Hands-On Tasks:** Watching a tutorial on a new cooking recipe while actually cooking can be an effective pairing. Similarly, watching a DIY video while assembling a piece of furniture can streamline the process.

The key is to ensure that one task doesn't detract from the other, and both can be performed to satisfactory standards.

3. **The Power of Routine:** When tasks are combined regularly, they can gradually form a routine, reducing the cognitive load and enhancing efficiency. Once a routine is established, the

brain doesn't have to expend as much energy deciding what to do or how to do it; the pattern is already set.

For example, if every morning you start your day by listening to industry news while making breakfast, this combination becomes a habit. Over time, you'll likely find that you're able to retain and process the information from the news better, even as your breakfast-making becomes more efficient or varied.

Similarly, if you've established a routine where you always do a 10-minute clean-up of your workspace while winding down and summarizing your day's tasks, this combination can lead to a clearer workspace and a clearer mind without feeling like additional effort.

The beauty of routines is that they capitalize on the brain's ability to form habits. By consistently pairing tasks, the brain starts processing them as a single, more complex task, streamlining execution. Over time, this not only enhances productivity but can also reduce feelings of being overwhelmed or scattered, as the routine provides a known structure amidst the chaos of daily tasks.

In conclusion, the efficiency of task combination lies in judicious pairings based on cognitive demands, forming routines out of effective pairings, and continuously assessing the quality of output to ensure no task is compromised. Properly harnessed, task combination can be a powerful tool in the quest for maximum productivity.

Implementing Strategies for Thoughtless Productivity

In our pursuit of increased productivity and efficiency, we often encounter scenarios where multiple tasks vie for our attention. By embracing strategies that allow for optimal combination, or "thoughtless productivity," we can navigate our responsibilities more effectively. Here's how to achieve this:

1. **Task Batching:** At the heart of efficiency lies the principle of reducing unnecessary switches in our workflow. Every time we shift from one type of task to another, there's a cognitive "switching cost"– our brains need time to adjust to the new task, recalibrate our focus, and gather the resources necessary for it.

   Task batching, or grouping similar tasks together, minimizes these switching costs. It operates on the principle that doing like tasks in a contiguous block is more efficient than sporadically doing them throughout the day.

For instance, consider email. Rather than responding to emails intermittently, it's often more productive to set aside specific blocks of time—perhaps once in the morning and once in the afternoon—to handle all email correspondence. During these periods, your mind is solely focused on that one type of task, maximizing efficiency.

Similarly, if you have several calls to make, it's beneficial to allocate a specific timeframe to make all these calls consecutively. By doing so, you streamline the process, setting up your workspace and mindset just once for a type of task, rather than multiple times throughout the day.

2. **Prioritization within Combination:** While combining tasks can be efficient, it's crucial to ensure that the main tasks receive the necessary focus. When combining, there should always be a hierarchy: a primary task that requires more cognitive focus and a secondary one that can be done more passively.

   For example, if you're attending a webinar (primary task) and decide to clean your desk simultaneously (secondary task), it's vital that the webinar content remains your priority. If a crucial point is being discussed, it might be wise to momentarily pause your cleaning, ensuring you fully absorb the information.

The danger lies in letting secondary tasks overshadow primary ones. It's easy to get carried away with a task that might be more engaging or provides a quicker sense of accomplishment, but always keep the hierarchy in mind.

3. **Recognizing Limits:** The human brain, despite its marvels, has limitations. While the idea of combining tasks can be enticing, there are moments when single-tasking is the only way to ensure a job is done right. This is particularly true for tasks that demand high cognitive engagement, creativity, or precision.

   For instance, if you're working on a critical project report, trying to listen to a podcast simultaneously could be counterproductive. The podcast might divert your attention, leading to errors in the report or a diluted understanding of the podcast's content.

   It's essential to be self-aware and recognize when the costs of multitasking outweigh the benefits. In scenarios where precision, creativity, or deep understanding is paramount, dedicating undivided attention is often the best strategy.

In conclusion, while thoughtless productivity strategies like task batching, prioritization within combination, and multitasking have their merits, they're tools in a toolkit. Knowing when and how to use them—while also recognizing their limitations—can pave the way for a more productive, efficient, and fulfilling work experience.

Harnessing Thoughtless Productivity: Examples, Lessons, and Avoiding Pitfalls

Individuals:

Example 1: **Language Learning during Commutes** Many individuals spend a significant amount of time commuting. Instead of seeing this as wasted time, some turn it into an opportunity for thoughtless productivity by listening to language learning tapes or apps.

Lesson Learned: Consistent exposure, even in passive contexts like a commute, can lead to substantial skill acquisition over time.

Pitfall to Avoid: Not choosing a quality language program or not being consistent in listening can result in limited progress. Also, ensure it doesn't distract from primary tasks, like driving.

Example 2: **Exercise while Watching TV** Many people have treadmills or stationary bikes at home. Instead of dedicating separate times for exercise and relaxation, they combine the two by exercising while watching their favorite shows.

Lesson Learned: Combining an activity that requires less cognitive engagement (like walking) with one that is more passive (watching TV) can lead to increased productivity without feeling overwhelmed.

Pitfall to Avoid: Safety first. Ensure that the setup is safe and that you don't get so engrossed in the show that you compromise your posture or pace.

Example 3: **Audiobooks during Household Chores** Instead of music, many individuals listen to audiobooks or informative podcasts while doing household chores, turning routine tasks into educational moments.

Lesson Learned: Mundane tasks can be made more engaging and productive with the addition of an educational component.

Pitfall to Avoid: Choose content that doesn't demand deep, reflective thinking when pairing with tasks that need attention, like cooking, to avoid accidents or oversights.

Companies:

Example 1: **Background Task Automation** Many companies use software that automates repetitive tasks (like data entry). Employees can initiate these processes and let them run in the background while focusing on other work.

Lesson Learned: Automation can dramatically improve efficiency and allow employees to focus on more value-added tasks.

Pitfall to Avoid: Over-reliance on automation without periodic checks can lead to errors going unnoticed. Ensure there's a balance between automation and manual oversight.

Example 2: **Scheduled Social Media Breaks** Some progressive companies, realizing that employees will periodically check their social media, have incorporated short, scheduled social media breaks. This allows employees a mental break and can improve overall concentration.

Lesson Learned: Recognizing and structuring inevitable habits can turn potential distractions into rejuvenating breaks.

Pitfall to Avoid: The key is moderation. Too many breaks or overly extended periods can harm productivity. It's essential to set clear guidelines.

Example 3: **Standing Meetings** To make meetings more efficient, some companies have adopted "standing meetings." The discomfort of standing ensures that the meeting stays concise and to the point.

Lesson Learned: Adjusting the environment or format of tasks can lead to increased efficiency.

Pitfall to Avoid: It's essential to ensure that the format doesn't exclude anyone, such as those with disabilities that might find standing for extended periods challenging.

In conclusion, both individuals and companies can harness thoughtless productivity with strategic task combinations and slight adjustments to their routine. The key lies in selecting complementary tasks, being consistent, and being aware of potential pitfalls to achieve the best outcomes.

Conclusion

In our ceaseless quest to achieve more in an ever-demanding world, the allure of multitasking often seems like an obvious solution. Yet, as we've delved into throughout this discussion, not all forms of multitasking are created equal. Thoughtless productivity emerges as a nuanced, strategic approach to combining tasks—allowing us to achieve more without the mental burnout commonly associated with traditional multitasking.

The significance of thoughtless productivity cannot be overstated. In an era where time is a luxury and demands on our attention are manifold, the ability to harness moments of 'downtime' or merge complementary tasks effectively becomes not just a skill, but a necessity. Thoughtless productivity is not about mindlessly cramming activities into every waking moment. Instead, it's about optimizing our time, ensuring that each moment is spent in a manner that aligns with our broader goals and well-being.

Yet, with the myriad benefits of thoughtless productivity also come potential pitfalls. While the art of combining tasks can lead to greater efficiency, it's crucial to distinguish this from haphazard multitasking. The latter often results in spreading oneself too thin, leading to errors, decreased quality of output, and even mental fatigue. When multitasking is unplanned or forced, it often becomes counterproductive. The true power of thoughtless productivity lies in its deliberate nature—combining tasks that naturally fit together, without causing cognitive dissonance or stress.

For example, pairing a cognitive task with a physical one—like listening to a podcast while jogging—can be a form of effective thoughtless productivity. On the other hand, trying to write a report while participating in a crucial conference call can lead to mistakes in both tasks. The essence, then, is not in doing more things simultaneously but in pairing the right tasks for maximum efficiency and quality.

As with all strategies in life and work, the approach to productivity should not be static. The dynamic nature of our lives, with changing responsibilities, technologies, and even personal interests, means that the methods that work best for us today might not be as effective tomorrow. Continuous evaluation is key. Regularly reflect on how various combinations of tasks are affecting both the quality of your work and your mental state. Are you feeling more efficient, or just more rushed? Are the results of your efforts of a standard that you can be proud of?

In embracing thoughtless productivity, individuals are encouraged to maintain a balance. Celebrate the moments of increased efficiency, but also recognize when it's time to single-task and give something your undivided attention. The ultimate aim is not just to do more but to do better, all while maintaining mental well-being.

In conclusion, thoughtless productivity offers a promising avenue for those looking to optimize their time and efforts. However, it's not a panacea. It requires discernment, continuous evaluation, and, occasionally, the wisdom to know when to step back and focus solely on the task at hand. As you move forward, may you find the perfect balance in your productivity journey, achieving your goals while preserving the quality of both your work and your peace of mind.

CHAPTER 11

Front-end Loading

The Imperative of Front-End Loading: A Deep Dive

The **Core Problem**: In the realm of task and project management, timing and distribution of effort are pivotal. Often, the chronology of work allocation can dictate not just the quality of the outcome but also the overall experience of the process. Here lies the crux of the problem: *how should one allocate effort across a given time frame?*

Back-end Loading: The Reactive Scramble: Back-end loading, as the name suggests, concentrates effort towards the end of the allocated time. Initially, it might seem attractive, especially to habitual procrastinators, as it gives a deceptive sensation of ample time. But this is a classic manifestation of the *Student Syndrome*. As the deadline looms closer, the scramble intensifies. The resulting rush pushes tasks into the urgent quadrant of Covey's matrix. Here, reactive rather than proactive decisions dominate. There's little time for reflection, optimization, or iteration. Quality invariably takes a back seat as the focus shifts to merely getting it done. Moreover, if unforeseen issues (courtesy of Murphy's Law) pop up during this late stage, the task or project can become a catastrophe, compounded by stress and panic.

Uniform Loading: The Perils of Assumption: On paper, uniform loading sounds logical. Divide the task into equal parts across the available time. Yet, it operates on a precarious assumption: that our time estimation is both accurate and infallible. But reality often deviates from such ideal assumptions. Work complexities can vary, and unexpected hurdles can arise. If Murphy's Law strikes when 90% of the task is done, the remaining 10% can exponentially inflate, throwing off the entire "uniform" plan.

Front-End Loading: Proactivity and Preparedness: Front-end loading flips the script. By front-loading tasks, significant portions of the work are tackled at the outset. This approach is grounded in proactive management, allowing for thoughtful planning, execution, and revision if needed. The early completion of major components provides a buffer, a cushion against potential miscalculations in time estimates or unforeseen challenges. Even if Murphy's Law decides to intervene late in the process, the bulk of the work is already done, ensuring that deadlines are met without compromising on quality.

By emphasizing front-end loading, we create an environment conducive to thoughtful work while minimizing stress. It provides the leeway to address errors, make improvements, and still deliver on time. In essence, front-end loading isn't just a task management strategy; it's a philosophy that emphasizes preparedness, quality, and peace of mind.

Note: In the remainder of this chapter, we will look at Front-End Loading both in an individual context (task management) and a corporate context (project management). Front-End Loading is applicable in both contexts.

Impediments to Productivity and the Power of Front-End Loading

Introduction to Impediments: While time management strategies aim to enhance productivity, certain inherent behaviors and phenomena serve as barriers. Recognizing these impediments is the first step towards devising strategies to counteract them.

1. Procrastination:

- **Explanation**: This is the act of delaying or postponing tasks, usually stemming from a lack of motivation, fear of failure, or simply the preference for doing something more enjoyable.

- **Impact on Productivity**: Procrastination eats into the available time for task completion, reducing the overall efficiency and often leading to rushed work or missed deadlines. The deferred tasks tend to accumulate, creating a daunting backlog.

2. Student Syndrome:

- **Explanation**: Derived from the observation that students tend to start their work right at the brink of a deadline, it refers to the act of delaying the start of a task until its due date is imminent.

- **Impact on Productivity**: Like procrastination, it results in a rushed job, often sacrificing the quality of work. The last-minute scramble can lead to errors and omissions.

3. Parkinson's Law:

- **Explanation**: "Work expands to fill the time available for its completion." Essentially, if you give a task more time than it requires, it will take that entire duration, often due to overthinking, overcomplicating, or over-perfecting it.

- **Impact on Productivity**: By allowing tasks to consume more time than necessary, other tasks can get sidelined, leading to inefficient time usage.

4. Murphy's Law:

- **Explanation**: "Anything that can go wrong will go wrong." While not a universal truth, it's a cautionary principle suggesting that unforeseen challenges can and will arise.

- **Impact on Productivity**: Unexpected hitches can derail the progress of a task, causing delays and disruptions. If not prepared, these can push tasks beyond their deadlines.

Countering Impediments with Front-End Loading: Front-end loading emerges as an antidote to these productivity barriers. By tackling significant portions of tasks at the onset, there's a minimized need to procrastinate as the task's momentum is already set. It discourages the Student Syndrome since the task has begun well before the deadline looms. In terms of Parkinson's

Law, front-loading ensures that the task doesn't unduly stretch, as the emphasis is on swift and efficient completion from the start. Lastly, by having a substantial part of the task done early, Murphy's Law's effects are mitigated. Even if unforeseen challenges arise, there's a buffer time to address them without compromising the deadline or quality.

The Importance of Completing Significant Parts of Tasks First

In the realm of time management and productivity, understanding the components of a task is crucial. This brings us to the concept of the 'significant parts' of a task. But what does this mean?

Defining 'Significant Parts': When we talk about the significant parts of a task, we're distinguishing the pivotal components– the core elements that define the task's essence and are paramount to its completion– from the peripheral or supplementary ones. Think of it as distinguishing between the foundation and framework of a house versus its paint or decorative elements. The former is integral for the structure, while the latter enhances it.

Benefits:

- **Better Task Management**: By addressing the major components first, there's a strategic sequencing in play. This early focus ensures the task's foundation is solid, making the subsequent stages smoother and more efficient. The outcome is not just completion but completion with precision.

- **Overcoming the Tendencies to Delay**: Front-loading tasks by tackling the significant parts initially serves as a powerful antidote to procrastination. It steers clear of the dangers of the Student Syndrome, where tasks are delayed until the eleventh hour, often at the cost of quality. It also combats the inefficiencies that come with Parkinson's Law, where work stretches to fit the time allotted.

- **Defence Against Murphy's Law**: As the saying goes, "Anything that can go wrong will go wrong." However, front-end loading acts as a buffer against this. When a substantial portion of a task is accomplished upfront, unforeseen challenges later on have a diminished impact. It's the principle of being better safe than sorry in action.

Real-life Examples: In the business world, consider a company launching a new product. If the research, design, and prototype testing (significant parts) are addressed at the outset, later challenges in marketing or distribution (peripheral components) can be handled with more agility. Similarly, in academic projects, commencing with thorough research and a structured outline ensures that subsequent stages like writing and proofreading are streamlined. These instances underscore the tangible benefits of prioritizing essential components from the get-go.

Steps and Benefits of Front-end Loading

Front-end Loading Defined

Front-end Loading (FEL) is a strategic approach in project management and task execution where significant resources, efforts, and attention are disproportionately allocated to the initial stages or phases of a project or task. This method prioritizes addressing the most critical components at the outset, ensuring that foundational elements are robustly established before progressing further. FEL is rooted in the belief that a strong beginning, where vital aspects are dealt with upfront, not only sets the tone for the remainder of the project but also mitigates potential challenges, inefficiencies, and risks that may arise in later stages. By front-loading resources and focus, this approach aims to enhance overall project outcomes, streamline execution, and minimize last-minute adjustments or corrections.

Step-by-Step Guide to Front-end Loading

Assessment: The first step in front-end loading involves a meticulous evaluation of the task or project in hand. Here, the primary aim is to dissect the task into its core components, distinguishing the vital elements from the less significant ones. It's akin to mapping out a journey, where one identifies the main roads and landmarks. Understanding these critical components is foundational, as it sets the tone for the subsequent steps, ensuring that the initial efforts are channeled in the right direction.

Scheduling: Once the essential components are clear, the next stage involves allocating sufficient time at the beginning to tackle these elements. This proactive allocation ensures that the pivotal parts get the focus, energy, and resources they deserve right from the start, minimizing the chances of last-minute scrambles and oversights.

Monitoring: As the task progresses, it's paramount to keep a close watch on the developments, especially during the early stages. Monitoring involves routinely checking the progress of the identified crucial components to ensure they are being addressed as planned. This step acts as a quality control measure, ensuring that the initial efforts are yielding the desired outcomes and that the task's foundation is being laid solidly.

Adapting: Even with meticulous assessment, scheduling, and monitoring, challenges can emerge. The ability to adapt becomes crucial at this juncture. Based on the progress checks from the monitoring stage, if discrepancies or unforeseen hurdles arise, adjustments need to be made. This might involve reallocating resources, tweaking the approach, or even revisiting the assessment stage to ensure nothing was overlooked. Adaptation ensures that the front-end loading approach remains dynamic and responsive to real-time challenges.

Benefits of FEL

Enhanced Quality: One of the standout benefits of the Front-end Loading approach is the notable improvement in the overall quality of work. When critical components of a task or project receive early and dedicated attention, it ensures that these foundational elements are thoroughly addressed and honed. This meticulousness in the beginning stages ensures that subsequent work builds upon a solid foundation, thereby enhancing the final output's quality and coherence.

Reduced Stress: A significant advantage of employing FEL is the reduction in work-related stress. Instead of the anxiety that typically accompanies last-minute rushes and the scramble to meet looming deadlines, FEL promotes a more evenly distributed workload. By addressing pivotal elements upfront, the pressure towards the end of a project is considerably alleviated, leading to a more balanced and less stress-inducing work experience.

Efficient Resource Utilization: Front-end Loading is not just about time; it's about optimally utilizing all available resources. By concentrating efforts at the beginning, resources such as finances, manpower, and equipment are used more efficiently. This intentional early allocation ensures that resources are not wasted or spread thin in later stages, leading to better outcomes with potentially reduced costs.

Anticipation of Challenges: FEL inherently possesses a proactive nature. Dedicating focused efforts during the initial stages allows teams and individuals to identify potential challenges or roadblocks earlier in the process. This early identification means that there is more time to develop solutions, make necessary adjustments, or even recalibrate the entire approach if needed. As a result, projects are less likely to face significant disruptions or setbacks, ensuring smoother execution and more predictable results.

Examples of Front-end Loading (FEL)

1. **Construction Projects:** In the realm of construction, FEL can be seen when significant efforts are made during the planning and design phases. Detailed blueprints are prepared, feasibility studies conducted, and thorough site analyses are performed before actual construction

begins. By front-loading these vital activities, it becomes easier to anticipate challenges like unsuitable terrains, potential permit issues, or design flaws, ensuring smoother construction later on.

2. **Software Development**: In software development, a project often starts with intensive requirement gathering, user research, and architectural design. These upfront efforts ensure that the developed software aligns well with user needs and that potential challenges in integration or scalability are addressed before coding begins.

3. **Event Planning**: When organizing an event, if logistics, venue bookings, and major attractions or speakers are locked in well in advance, it leaves room to handle promotional activities, RSVPs, and other finer details with greater attention and reduced rush as the event date approaches.

Pointers for Effective Front-end Loading

- **Detailed Research**: Before diving into the task, invest time in understanding all its facets. Knowledge is power when deciding which parts to front-load.

- **Stakeholder Engagement**: Engage with all stakeholders early to gather their inputs and requirements. This ensures everyone's needs are considered from the start.

- **Regular Reviews**: Conduct periodic reviews to ensure that the front-loaded tasks are progressing as planned and making the desired impact.

Conclusion

Front-end Loading is more than just a time management strategy; it's a philosophy that champions proactiveness, foresight, and strategic thinking. By concentrating efforts and resources on the early phases of a project, not only are better outcomes often achieved, but the entire process becomes more streamlined and less stressful. While the immediate allure of FEL is the promise of better quality and efficiency, its true power lies in its ability to make projects more predictable and manageable. As with any approach, the key to successful FEL lies in understanding its principles, adapting it to the task at hand, and continuously refining the process based on feedback and results. Embracing Front-end Loading can indeed be a transformative decision, steering projects towards success and offering a clearer path through the myriad challenges of task and project management.

CHAPTER 12

Early Deadlines

Introduction: The Jesse Owens Inspiration

The 1936 Olympics held in Berlin is memorable for a plethora of reasons, not the least of which was the indomitable spirit and talent of Jesse Owens. But among his many triumphs, there is a particular story that serves as a metaphorical touchstone for the transformative power of imaginary deadlines.

Jesse Owens, a favored contender for the long jump gold medal, faced an unforeseen challenge during the heats. His initial attempts were riddled with errors: a foot fault on the first jump and an oversight on the second, where he ran past the jump-off line. It seemed that a promising medal prospect was on the verge of a disheartening elimination.

But then, a remarkable gesture from an unexpected quarter turned things around. Luz Long, Owens' German competitor, approached him with a suggestion that would prove invaluable. He advised Owens to envision a jump-off line several inches before the actual one. Owens embraced this notion of an "imaginary" line, allowing him to qualify with ease. Energized and refocused, he later executed a jump that not only secured him the gold medal but also set a new world record.

This story, often celebrated as an emblem of sportsmanship during a politically charged event, also underscores another potent message: the magic of setting and believing in an "imaginary" marker. Just as Owens used that imagined line to propel himself to victory, setting early, self-imposed deadlines in our tasks can catalyze our productivity and success.

The Psychology Behind Setting Deadlines

Deadlines have an uncanny ability to bring clarity, urgency, and focus to our actions. The tick-tock of an approaching deadline, whether set by oneself or by external forces, has a tangible effect on our psyche, influencing our behavior and driving us to act. But what is it about deadlines that evoke such a potent response?

For starters, a deadline acts as a commitment device. When we commit to completing a task within a specific timeframe, it often establishes a psychological contract. We then begin to allocate our resources, be it time, effort, or cognitive bandwidth, to meet this self-imposed or externally set agreement. This contract, in many ways, keeps us accountable. It brings forth a vision of an end, an impending point in time by which our efforts should culminate into a tangible result. And with this vision, our mind shifts from the passive mode of intention to the active mode of execution.

Moreover, the human psyche has an innate behavior, quite paradoxical, where it often tailors the duration of a task based on the time available. As articulated by Parkinson's Law, "Work expands to fill the time available for its completion." Given too much time, we might find ourselves lingering, overanalyzing, or sometimes even procrastinating. But introduce a deadline into this equation, and suddenly, the nebulous task becomes more structured. We start strategizing, prioritizing, and often innovating to meet the end goal within the stipulated time.

However, while deadlines provide direction and can be a valuable tool to spur action, they can also introduce stress, especially if they seem unrealistic or if they are approached without a proper strategy. This brings us to the magic of setting "imaginary" or early deadlines– a concept that borrows from Jesse Owens' Olympic tale but finds relevance in our daily endeavors. By tricking our minds to believe in an earlier deadline, we can harness the focus and urgency it introduces while still leaving buffer time to account for unforeseen challenges.

The Self-deception Prerequisite

At the heart of harnessing the magic of early deadlines lies an intriguing and counterintuitive proposition: one must willingly and consciously deceive oneself. This notion of self-deception, while it may seem paradoxical, holds the key to unlocking the effectiveness of imaginary deadlines.

The psychology of self-deception is a complex tapestry interwoven with our desires, beliefs, and actions. To deceive oneself is not merely to believe a lie, but to live it, to embed it in one's psyche so deeply that it influences behavior. But why would anyone choose to believe something that isn't real, especially when they themselves are the architect of that very falsehood?

The answer lies in the outcome. Just as a placebo can sometimes induce real physiological responses, the belief in an early deadline can drive real productivity outcomes. The mind, convinced of the falsehood, directs our actions as though the imagined deadline were real, instilling a sense of urgency, focus, and determination that might otherwise be absent.

Yet, embracing such self-deception is no trivial endeavor. It requires a delicate balance. On one hand, we're aware of the artifice, having set the imaginary deadline ourselves. On the other, we must immerse ourselves in the belief so thoroughly that our conscious mind accepts the early deadline as the actual one.' It is this belief that bestows upon the imaginary deadline its potency. If regarded merely as a soft target or a tentative date, the effectiveness of the strategy diminishes. Instead of a compelling motivator, it becomes a suggestion that's easily overlooked or dismissed.

Thus, the crux of employing early deadlines successfully hinges on our ability to straddle this duality: the knowledge of the deception and the genuine belief in its truth. It's a conscious commitment to an illusion, with the understanding that this illusion, when truly believed, can be a powerful catalyst for action.

Advantages of Having an Imaginary Deadline

Enhanced Productivity: One of the most tangible benefits of setting an imaginary deadline is the notable uptick in productivity.

With the clock seemingly ticking faster, there's a heightened motivation to focus on the task at hand and bring it to completion. The mind perceives a shorter timeframe, pushing us to allocate resources more efficiently and reduce unnecessary delays. As a result, tasks often reach completion faster than they might have with a more distant, real deadline.

Buffer Time: Setting an earlier deadline affords an invaluable cushion of time post task completion. This buffer can be utilized in myriad ways: refining the work, adding finishing touches, thorough reviewing, or simply ensuring everything is in perfect order. Additionally, should any unexpected challenges or obstacles arise, this buffer ensures they can be addressed without encroaching upon the actual deadline, preserving the quality and integrity of the task.

Reduced Stress: The anxiety associated with looming deadlines is a sentiment many are familiar with. By working with an imaginary deadline that precedes the real one, individuals often finish their tasks well in advance, thereby sidestepping the typical rush and stress of last-minute scrambles. This proactive approach leads to a more serene and controlled work process, minimizing potential errors that can arise from hasty, stressed efforts.

Increased Creativity: Contrary to what one might expect, an impending deadline doesn't always stifle creativity; sometimes, it catalyzes it. An immediate sense of urgency can ignite the brain, prompting innovative solutions and ideas. When confronted with the challenge of a rapidly approaching (albeit imaginary) deadline, the mind can surprise with its capacity to think outside the box, producing unique and inventive results.

Flexibility: Beyond the tangible benefits of quality and timeliness, an imaginary deadline offers a more intangible advantage: flexibility. Life is unpredictable, and unforeseen urgencies can crop up without warning. By working towards an earlier deadline, there's room to maneuver, ensuring that even if something urgent diverts attention or resources, the actual deadline isn't compromised. This built-in flexibility allows for a more adaptable and resilient approach to tasks.

Setting and Sticking to Early Deadlines

Visible Reminders: In an age of information overload, it's easy for deadlines to get lost amidst a flurry of other commitments. To ensure that an early deadline doesn't slip through the cracks, it's essential to have visible reminders. Tools like digital calendars, sticky notes on computer monitors, or comprehensive to-do lists can be instrumental. Not only do they keep the deadline at the forefront of your mind, but they also serve as a constant nudge, pushing you towards completion before the deadline.

Accountability: There's something about external awareness that amplifies commitment. By sharing your early deadline with a colleague, friend, or supervisor, you create an external point of accountability. Knowing that someone else is aware of your intended completion date can serve as a powerful motivator. It's not just about meeting the deadline for yourself, but also about living up to the expectation you've set in front of others.

Reward Mechanism: Behavioral science often cites positive reinforcement as an effective way to encourage desired behaviors. Applying this principle to early deadlines, you can establish a reward mechanism for yourself. Whether it's a treat, a short break, or something larger, having a self-reward in place for meeting the early deadline can serve as a tangible motivation, making you more likely to stick to the advanced timeline.

Regular Check-ins: One of the pitfalls of setting an early deadline is the risk of becoming complacent. To counter this, it's beneficial to have routine progress reviews. These don't have to be extensive; even a quick daily assessment of where you stand concerning the early deadline can be enough. It ensures that you remain aligned with your goal and can make necessary adjustments if you find yourself veering off track.

Feedback Loop: After you've completed the task, take a moment to reflect. Was the early deadline realistic? Did it provide the anticipated benefits? Was it too lenient or perhaps too aggressive? Creating a feedback loop where you evaluate the effectiveness of the early deadline allows for continuous improvement. By adjusting based on past experiences, you refine your approach, ensuring that with each subsequent task, your proficiency in setting and sticking to early deadlines only enhances.

Conclusion

The power of setting imaginary deadlines finds its most poignant representation in the story of Jesse Owens. Standing at a crossroads of potential failure and historic achievement in the 1936 Olympics, Owens drew from the wisdom imparted by Luz Long, and the rest, as they say, is history. This tale not only underscores the significance of an imaginary jump-off line but also showcases the monumental outcomes such seemingly simple strategies can herald.

In the realm of productivity, the early deadline technique hinges on a unique paradox. It's an act of deliberate self-deception—of making oneself believe in a falsehood, but to a beneficial end. By wholeheartedly embracing these self-set imaginary deadlines, we unlock levels of efficiency, focus, and drive that might otherwise remain dormant.

The key lies in genuinely committing to these constructed timelines, allowing them to guide our workflow as any real deadline would. This approach, paradoxical as it may seem, has the potential to revolutionize how we handle tasks, ensuring that we consistently deliver not just on time but ahead of it.

So, as we step forward, let's take inspiration from Owens and Long. Let's set our own imaginary jump-off lines, those early deadlines, and leverage their power to transform our daily endeavors. By doing so, we don't just complete tasks; we set the stage for unprecedented accomplishments and excellence in all we undertake.

CHAPTER 13

Buffer Management

Introduction: The Need for Buffers

In the intricate dance of daily operations, whether personal or professional, time is both a resource and a constraint. Each task we embark upon, no matter how well-charted, is fraught with variables and potential disruptions. This uncertainty and unpredictability in task durations arise from various factors-unexpected complexities, external interferences, or even our own fluctuating productivity levels.

Consider tasks as journeys. No matter how familiar the route, there's always a chance of unexpected roadblocks, detours, or delays. In the same vein, even a task we've performed multiple times can throw up surprises. An email that was supposed to take 5 minutes might spiral into a 30-minute task because of an unforeseen complication. A meeting slated for an hour might extend further due to unanticipated discussions.

Not accounting for these unpredictable elements is akin to setting oneself up for failure. Imagine a day packed back-to-back with tasks, with no room for overflows. One unexpected delay, and the entire day's schedule might cascade into chaos. The result? Missed deadlines, compromised quality, and mounting stress.

This is where buffers come into play. They act as safety nets, ensuring that when (not if) disruptions occur, we have a cushion to fall back on, a reservoir of time to draw from. They're not just an acknowledgment of the unpredictability of tasks but are essential tools for effective time management.

The Paradox of Padding Every Task

At first glance, it might seem prudent to add a buffer to every task we undertake. After all, by accounting for uncertainties in each task's duration, we ostensibly prepare ourselves for every eventuality. However, this approach brings with it an ironic and counterintuitive challenge: the very act of adding buffers to each task can lead to inefficiencies, and in many cases, even prolong the task unnecessarily.

Enter Parkinson's Law, a rather astute observation that "work expands to fill the time available for its completion." In essence, when we allocate more time to a task than it might genuinely need, there's an inherent human tendency to use up that entire duration, regardless of the task's actual complexity. The task, aware of its luxurious expanse of time, languorously stretches to occupy the entire window we've given it. What could have been completed in an hour, when given two hours, somehow still ends up consuming the full two hours.

So, what happens when we pad every task with additional buffer time? We inadvertently invite Parkinson's Law to each of those tasks. Instead of becoming more efficient, we might find ourselves, paradoxically, becoming less so. Each task swells, consuming its buffer, and often, there's no real productivity gain to show for that extra time.

In essence, by over-buffering, we're not genuinely preparing for uncertainties; we're merely diluting our focus and efficiency. We create an illusion of preparedness while potentially compromising on our productivity.

Goldratt's Insight into Buffering

Eliyahu Goldratt, known for his groundbreaking methodologies in operational efficiency, introduced a fresh perspective on task buffering. Rather than perceiving every task as a potential time overrun culprit, he presented a more nuanced and statistically supported viewpoint.

Goldratt observed that not all tasks within a set possess an equal risk of extending beyond their expected completion times. Instead of indiscriminately viewing each task as a potential delay source, he postulated that only a select fraction truly overstep their anticipated durations. This assertion isn't merely anecdotal but finds its roots in solid statistical analysis.

Digging into the numbers, if we examine a sample of 10 tasks, approximately 3, or more whimsically put, precisely 31.622776% of them, would require buffer time. This statistical insight means that a surprising 7 out of those 10 tasks (or 68.377224%, if we're playing with precision) would most likely finish within or even before their allocated time. This revelation disrupts the conventional wisdom of buffering every task, suggesting that such a strategy might be inadvertently inviting Parkinson's Law into play more often than we'd like.

With Goldratt's lens, we see a smarter way to approach buffering. Recognizing the inherent variability in tasks and armed with the knowledge that just about 31.622776% of tasks might demand a time cushion, planners can strategize with greater efficiency, ensuring buffers are employed where they're genuinely needed, rather than blanketing every task with unnecessary extra time.

Buffering Techniques: The 30% Rule

In the realm of task management and efficient planning, the introduction of buffers can either act as a strategic lifesaver or, when misapplied, an unnecessary drag on productivity. Goldratt's innovative approach provides an enlightening take on how to smartly apply buffers, and central to this approach is the 30% rule.

Rather than individually padding every task with its own buffer, a practice which can inefficiently bloat timelines, the 30% rule advocates for a collective approach. Here's how it works: When we group a set of tasks- say, a batch of 10- instead of allocating a buffer to each one, we determine a combined buffer for the entire group. But instead of this buffer being the total of all individual task buffers, it's streamlined to just 30% of that combined total. The genius of this technique becomes evident when you consider the resultant efficiency: a whopping 70% savings in buffer time.

The underlying logic is rooted in Goldratt's observation that only around 3 out of every 10 tasks are likely to overrun their estimated completion time. So, by setting aside a consolidated 30% buffer for the group, we're sufficiently prepared for those unexpected delays, while at the same time preventing the needless inflation of our schedule.

Mathematically, this approach is an optimization marvel. It aligns buffer allocation with the actual statistical likelihood of delays, ensuring that our projects remain both flexible and efficient. The 30% rule, in essence, provides a structured yet adaptable cushion, guaranteeing that projects can accommodate unforeseen challenges without drowning in excessive, unutilized buffer time.

Dummy Buffer Tasks: The Buffer Reservoir

In the intricate choreography of task management, envisioning buffer time as a tangible "reservoir" can be transformative. By creating a "dummy" task that holds this collective buffer, we not only neatly compartmentalize the reserve time but also gain a clearer perspective on how much buffer remains as tasks progress.

Imagine this dummy buffer task as a bank. Every time one of the grouped tasks overshoots its expected completion time, you "withdraw" the needed minutes or hours from this buffer bank.

However, just as with any loan, this borrowed time comes with the implicit understanding of repayment. Instead of monetary interest, the "interest" here is efficiency. To compensate for the time drawn from the buffer, subsequent tasks should aim for heightened efficiency, striving to be completed slightly ahead of schedule. This act of "repaying" ensures the buffer reservoir remains sufficiently stocked and prevents the buffer from depleting prematurely.

But what if you excel in this repayment? If tasks are consistently completed with heightened efficiency, not only does the buffer remain untouched, but additional time might also be "earned" back. This extra time can be a gateway to addressing standby tasks- those tasks lined up for the future, but not scheduled for the immediate day. With this proactive approach, today's efficiency yields tomorrow's free time. As standby tasks are tackled ahead of schedule, the cumulative effect can be substantial. Over time, the combination of front-loaded productivity and a well-maintained buffer reservoir might just open up enough free slots in your calendar for that long-desired vacation. In essence, through diligent buffer management and efficiency, we're not just meeting deadlines; we're crafting a future with more available time.

Advantages of Effective Buffer Management

Increased Productivity: One of the most immediate benefits of adept buffer management is a noticeable uptick in productivity. By consolidating buffer times and ensuring that only essential overflows tap into these reserves, a larger chunk of time becomes accessible for actual task execution. This means that not only are tasks getting done within their designated windows, but there may also be surplus time to address additional tasks. The result is a workday where more objectives are met, goals are achieved faster, and the overall output is heightened.

Reduced Stress: Operating without a buffer is akin to walking a tightrope without a safety net. The slightest miscalculation or unexpected delay can throw plans into disarray, leading to mounting stress. Effective buffer management acts as this much-needed safety net. With a well-maintained buffer reservoir in place, the anxiety associated with potential overruns is significantly diminished. Individuals can tackle tasks with the peace of mind that there's a cushion to fall back on should things not go precisely as planned.

Enhanced Efficiency: Buffer management isn't just about having a contingency plan; it's about maximizing the utility of every available minute. By honing the skill of grouping tasks and judiciously allocating buffers, wasted buffer durations become a thing of the past. Each moment is accounted for, either as productive work time or as a necessary buffer. This meticulous orchestration ensures that the available time is utilized to its utmost potential, leading to an overall boost in efficiency.

Practical Tips for Implementing Buffer Management

Grouping Tasks Effectively: The essence of buffer management lies in the ability to group tasks in a way that makes the most of combined buffer times. Start by categorizing tasks based on their nature, duration, and priority. Tasks that are similar in nature or those that follow a sequential order can be grouped together. For instance, if you have several writing assignments, it might make sense to group them since they require a similar frame of mind. Grouping tasks not only streamlines the process but also makes it easier to allocate a collective buffer time, ensuring you don't overcompensate with excessive individual buffers.

Monitoring and Adjusting Buffers: As with any strategy, the key to effective buffer management is constant monitoring and real-time adjustments. As tasks progress, keep a close eye on their adherence to allocated timeframes. If a particular task is taking longer than anticipated, draw from the buffer reservoir. However, this should also prompt a reassessment of subsequent tasks in that group. If one task has consumed a significant portion of the buffer, it may be wise to revisit and possibly adjust the buffer allocation for the remaining tasks, ensuring there's adequate buffer time left for any other unexpected delays.

Utilizing Tools and Software: In today's digital age, there's an abundance of tools and software designed to assist with time management, many of which have features tailored for buffer management. Tools like Trello, Asana, or Microsoft Project allow users to set tasks, assign durations, and incorporate buffers. These platforms also offer visual representations of tasks, making it easier to gauge progress and buffer consumption. Moreover, notifications and reminders can be set up to alert users when tasks are nearing their completion time or when buffers are being used up. By leveraging such tools, the intricacies of buffer management can be handled more efficiently, ensuring that the strategy is implemented consistently and effectively.

Conclusion: Embracing Smart Buffering

Effective time management is more than just allotting a set duration for tasks. It recognizes the inherent uncertainties and unpredictable nature of work and life, and this is where the art of buffering comes into play. By understanding the principles and benefits of buffer management, individuals and organizations can navigate the often tumultuous waters of task management with greater ease and confidence.

The essence of smart buffering is not about mere time allocation but in achieving a harmonious balance between dedicated task time and the reserved buffer. This balance ensures that we don't succumb to the pitfalls of Parkinson's Law, where tasks unnecessarily expand to fill the time allocated, nor do we fall victim to unexpected delays without a safety net.

However, as with all time management strategies, the effectiveness of buffer management is dependent on continual reflection, evaluation, and adjustment. As tasks evolve and unforeseen challenges emerge, so should our approach to buffering. It's a dynamic strategy, one that demands our attention and finesse.

In embracing smart buffering, we don't just aim for completing tasks but aim for efficiency, quality, and peace of mind. And in the long run, it's not just about getting things done, but about achieving more with less stress and greater satisfaction.

PART III:

ADAPTING TO THE UNPREDICTABLE

In our pursuit of efficiency and productivity, we often forget a fundamental truth about life: it is inherently unpredictable. No matter how meticulous our plans, unforeseen challenges can and often do emerge, compelling us to adapt and recalibrate. This section delves into understanding this unpredictability and equipping ourselves with strategies to navigate it with grace and efficiency.

Chapter 14: Life as an Unpredictable Game Drawing a vivid analogy with dodgeball, this chapter paints a picture of life's inherent unpredictability. Just as players must dodge, duck, and dive to avoid balls from unexpected directions, we too must navigate the curveballs life throws our way. The chapter explores the multiple dimensions of unpredictability: from known points of failure with uncertain timing, completely unknown points of failure, to the sudden external disruptions that can throw our plans off course.

Chapter 15: Tactics to Tackle the Unexpected While unpredictability is a given, how we respond to it can make all the difference. This chapter offers a suite of tactics designed to help us tackle the unexpected with finesse. Firstly, the chapter sheds light on the art of re-prioritization, guiding us on distinguishing between urgency and importance and providing methods to efficiently reorder our tasks. As we move forward, we'll learn the nuances of shuffling tasks around, aided by modern digital tools. Recognizing our limits and preventing overburden is pivotal, and the chapter emphasizes strategies to ensure we don't bite off more than we can chew. Lastly, at the heart of it all, lies our mindset. The chapter concludes with psychological insights and practical advice on staying calm amidst the chaos and embracing the essential quality of flexibility in our time management journey.

CHAPTER 14

Life as an Unpredictable Game

L ife, in many ways, mirrors a game of dodgeball. In this fast-paced, chaotic game, players are continually on their toes, making snap judgments, and responding to balls thrown from all directions. They might anticipate a ball coming from the left, but suddenly one whizzes past from the right. The unpredictability of where and when the next ball will come keeps the players alert and adaptable. Similarly, life throws its challenges at us from unexpected quarters and often when we least expect them. It is this inherent unpredictability of life that makes our journey both exciting and challenging.

Known Points of Failure, Unknown Timing

The first dimension of unpredictability is similar to a dodgeball game where we know an opponent will throw the ball, but we don't know exactly when. In life, these are scenarios where we anticipate a challenge, but its timing remains elusive. For instance, anyone working in technology knows that systems can fail. They might have the best infrastructure in place, but they cannot predict the exact moment a server might crash or a piece of code might malfunction. A financial investor knows the markets are volatile, but cannot pinpoint the exact timing of the next recession. This kind of unpredictability requires a proactive mindset. Just as a dodgeball player remains vigilant, even when they can't see a ball coming, we too need to build systems, checks, and balances that help us respond swiftly when the anticipated challenge strikes.

Unknown Points of Failure

The second dimension is even more unpredictable. It's like playing dodgeball blindfolded. You don't know who will throw the ball, from where, or when. These are challenges in life that catch us completely off guard because we never saw them coming. A sudden health diagnosis, an unexpected job loss, or a relationship turning sour without warning are examples of such scenarios. These situations test our resilience and our ability to think on our feet. They remind us of the importance of cultivating a strong mental and emotional foundation, and having a reliable support system. Just as a blindfolded dodgeball player would rely heavily on their intuition and other senses, we too need to hone our instincts and strengthen other areas of our lives to navigate these unknown challenges.

External Disruptions

Lastly, there are external disruptions. In our dodgeball analogy, this would be like someone suddenly changing the rules of the game or introducing new players halfway through. In life, these disruptions come in the form of global events or changes in our external environment that we have little to no control over. The COVID-19 pandemic is a prime example. Overnight, individuals and businesses had to adapt to a new normal, rethinking how they live, work, and interact. Natural disasters, political upheavals, or technological breakthroughs also fall into this category. While we cannot control these disruptions, we can control our response. Adaptability, innovation, and a willingness to pivot become our greatest allies in such scenarios.

Conclusion

In conclusion, life's unpredictability, much like a game of dodgeball, is what keeps us engaged, alert, and evolving. While the challenges might seem daunting, they also offer opportunities for growth, learning, and transformation. By recognizing the dimensions of unpredictability and equipping ourselves to handle each type, we not only navigate life's challenges more efficiently but also transform them into stepping stones for success. As the saying goes, "It's not about avoiding the balls life throws at us, but learning how to dodge, catch, or throw them back."

CHAPTER 15

Tactics to Tackle the Unexpected

D espite our best-laid plans, life often throws curveballs. How we respond to these unexpected challenges defines our resilience and adaptability. This chapter arms you with pragmatic tactics to navigate through unexpected situations. From the art of re-prioritizing tasks, shuffling schedules, ensuring we don't overburden ourselves, to maintaining composure amidst chaos, we delve deep into strategies that ensure continuous productivity and mental equilibrium, no matter the circumstances.

Re-Prioritize

In an ever-changing landscape, our goals and objectives may need frequent readjustment. The ability to re-prioritize is a fundamental skill when faced with the unexpected. First, one needs to understand the twin concepts of importance and urgency. While urgent tasks demand immediate attention, important tasks align with our long-term goals. The challenge is discerning between what feels urgent and what truly is important.

To efficiently re-prioritize tasks, begin by categorizing them based on urgency and importance. Use the Eisenhower Box or Covey Quadrants as a method. Tasks that are both urgent and important take precedence. Those that are important but not urgent can be scheduled for later. Delegate or defer what is urgent but not important, and eliminate tasks that are neither.

Furthermore, set aside regular intervals, daily or weekly, to review your to-do list. The act of evaluation will keep you aligned with your goals, and allow you to adjust course when necessary.

Shuffle Things Around

Life's unpredictability might mean that your meticulously planned schedule needs rearranging. Start by identifying the tasks that have some flexibility in terms of deadlines. Next, pinpoint time slots that can accommodate these movable tasks.

Digital tools can be invaluable allies in this process. Calendar apps, like Google Calendar or Microsoft Outlook, allow for easy rescheduling, often with just a drag and drop. Task management apps, such as Todoist or Trello, provide visual aids to help gauge the workload and can be instrumental in reshuffling tasks based on priority.

Don't Overburden

In the face of unexpected events, there's a temptation to cram more tasks into an already packed schedule, leading to burnout. Recognizing one's limits is crucial. Overloading yourself not only affects the quality of your work but can also take a toll on mental and physical health.

To prevent burnout, make it a habit to periodically assess your workload. Are there tasks that can be deferred or delegated? Ensure to schedule breaks and downtime. Adopt techniques like the Pomodoro Technique, which mandates short breaks after intervals of focused work. Furthermore, be honest with yourself and others about what you can realistically achieve in a given timeframe.

Stay Calm and Adjust

The initial reaction to unexpected challenges is often stress or panic. However, emotional upheavals can cloud judgment and hamper decision-making. Adopting psychological approaches, like deep breathing exercises, mindfulness meditation, or simply taking a short walk, can help restore calm.

Flexibility, both in mindset and action, is at the core of navigating the unpredictable. Understand that plans are guidelines, not rigid structures. They should serve you, not constrain you. Embrace a growth mindset, viewing challenges as opportunities to learn and adapt. Cultivating this attitude will not only help you tackle the unexpected with grace but also turn potential setbacks into stepping stones for growth.

PART IV

TACTICAL TIME MANAGEMENT IN PRACTICE

In the realm of time management, a synthesis of traditional and tactical approaches can yield unparalleled efficiency. While the structured nature of traditional time management provides a solid foundation, the dynamic strategies of tactical time management allow for swift adaptation in the face of unforeseen challenges. This synergy, where the predictability of the traditional meets the adaptability of the tactical, offers a comprehensive strategy that maximizes efficiency and efficacy. In this part, we dive deep into the practical implementation of this combined approach, offering insights, exercises, and advice to master tactical time management in everyday scenarios.

Chapter 16: Planning with a Tactical Twist. Dive into the foundational aspects of traditional planning—structuring your week, setting overarching goals, and methodically breaking them down. But there's a twist: we infuse this systematic approach with the nimbleness of tactical time management. By integrating strategies like buffer times, early deadlines, and front-end loading, we'll showcase how to supercharge your planning regimen. Experience this synergy through the lens of a project manager who masterfully wields both approaches.

Chapter 17: Exercises for Mastery. Put theory into practice with exercises designed to hone your tactical time management skills. Tackle real-world scenarios to discern the optimal tactical techniques, audit a week of your activities to pinpoint areas of improvement, and challenge yourself with early deadline tasks to assess your proficiency.

Chapter 18: Practical Tips and Advice. Mastering tactical time management requires more than just theory—it's about practical application. Learn the value of adaptability, the importance of daily reflection, and the advantages of leveraging technology. Emphasize mindfulness, a crucial component that enhances your ability to swiftly shift gears when circumstances demand.

Chapter 19: The Role of Flexibility. Flexibility isn't just a virtue— it's a necessity in the dynamic landscape of modern life. Delve into the significance of a flexible mindset in time management and explore the balance between unwavering commitment to a plan and the agility to deviate when needed. Drawing from real-life anecdotes, discover the pitfalls of rigidity and the power of adaptability.

Embrace the confluence of these two worlds and witness a transformation in how you manage, allocate, and utilize your time.

Chapter 20 Summary: Embracing the Tactical. Chapter 20 serves as a comprehensive wrap-up of the themes discussed throughout the section. It underscores the pivotal role of amalgamating traditional time management techniques with tactical strategies, emphasizing the benefits this fusion brings. The chapter revisits crucial lessons and takeaways derived from real-life examples and practical exercises, ensuring readers can internalize and apply these insights in their daily lives. Lastly, the chapter projects a forward-looking view of time management, envisioning a shift from stringent methods to a more adaptive and fluid approach, underlining the essence of adaptability in the face of evolving challenges.

CHAPTER 16

Planning with a Tactical Twist

The Basics of Traditional Planning

Traditional planning serves as the backbone of effective time management. It is akin to laying the foundation for a building, where each brick represents a planned activity, and the mortar is the commitment to adhere to that plan. At the core of traditional planning lies the creation of weekly or monthly planners. These planners are systematic representations of how one envisions their time distribution over a specified period. They contain detailed schedules, allocated time slots for tasks, and often, overarching objectives for the respective duration.

Additionally, setting up goals is a pivotal aspect of this approach. These goals can be both short-term, like completing a specific project within a week, and long-term, like achieving a promotion in a year. Having well-defined goals offers direction and ensures that time is being spent purposefully. When you know where you're heading, your actions, tasks, and daily activities align with that vision, ensuring efficiency and progress.

Injecting Tactical Elements

While the structured approach of traditional planning is invaluable, it often lacks the flexibility to adjust to real-time challenges. This is where tactical time management comes into play, enhancing traditional planning with a more agile methodology.

One of the first tactical elements that can be incorporated is buffer times. By setting aside specific periods within the planner as "buffers," one can account for unforeseen delays or challenges. These buffers act as safety nets, ensuring that a single delay doesn't derail the entire plan.

Setting early deadlines is another tactical maneuver. Drawing from the principles discussed earlier, early deadlines encourage efficiency and prevent tasks from dragging on needlessly. This approach ensures tasks are completed well before their actual deadlines, providing ample time for revisions or to address unexpected hitches.

Front-end loading, or focusing on significant parts of bigger tasks at the onset, also aligns with tactical planning. This tactic ensures that primary components of projects are tackled early, leaving room for adjustments and refinements as the task progresses.

Example: A Week in the Life of a Project Manager

Let's envision a project manager named Alex. Alex's traditional planning approach would typically involve setting up a weekly planner, detailing meetings, setting milestones for the project, and allocating tasks to team members. Objectives for the week would be clear, like completing the design phase of a project.

However, using the combined approach, Alex begins by setting early deadlines. Instead of waiting for the team's input by the end of the week, Alex sets a mid-week review. This move ensures that any design discrepancies are caught early on.

Alex also front-loads tasks. The first two days of the week are heavily focused on brainstorming and initial design concepts, ensuring that the most crucial parts of the design phase are tackled when energy and enthusiasm are at their peak.

Lastly, Alex incorporates buffer times. Knowing the unpredictability of design work and potential for revisions, blocks of time are kept open in the schedule. When a design revision came up on Wednesday, instead of causing stress or pushing other tasks out of the way, Alex utilized the buffer, ensuring the rest of the week remained unaffected.

This combined approach not only allowed Alex to manage time more effectively but also ensured that the quality of work was high, team stress was minimized, and the project stayed on track.

CHAPTER 17

Exercises for Mastery

Scenario Practice

Explanation: Scenario practice involves presenting real-life situations or hypothetical, yet realistic, challenges to see how one would handle them using the tactical techniques learned. This exercise is akin to a flight simulator for pilots, offering a safe environment to test out strategies without real-world consequences.

How to Execute:

1. Develop or find a list of diverse scenarios that one might face in their professional or personal life. For instance, a project deadline moved up unexpectedly, an urgent task appearing out of nowhere, or having multiple tasks due at the same time.

2. Analyze each scenario and decide which tactical technique is best suited to handle it. Would front-end loading be helpful? Or perhaps an early deadline would drive efficiency? Maybe buffer time could alleviate some stress?

Outcome: The primary outcome of the scenario practice is enhanced decision-making. As one gets accustomed to thinking tactically in diverse situations, the ability to make swift and effective decisions in real-life challenges improves. This exercise essentially strengthens the tactical "muscle," ensuring that when faced with unpredictability, one has a well-practiced repertoire of strategies to employ.

Time Audit

Explanation: A time audit involves meticulous tracking of one's activities over a set period, often a week. The objective is to identify patterns, recognize time-wasters, and determine where tactical time management techniques might have improved efficiency.

How to Execute:

1. For one week, keep a detailed log of all activities. This includes work tasks, breaks, recreational activities, chores, and even unexpected interruptions.

2. At the end of the week, review the log. Identify periods where time could have been better managed or where disruptions caused significant delays.

3. Analyze these inefficiencies or disruptions and determine which tactical techniques could have been applied. Could a buffer have helped? Would front-end loading a task have made a difference?

Outcome: The time audit's outcome is twofold. Firstly, it offers a mirror, reflecting one's actual time usage versus perceived time management. It can be a revelation to see how much time is spent on unproductive activities or how often disruptions derail a day. Secondly, by identifying where tactical techniques could have been employed, it provides a roadmap for future improvement, ensuring better productivity and efficiency moving forward.

Early Deadline Challenge

Explanation: The Early Deadline Challenge pushes individuals to set deadlines ahead of the actual due date. The aim is to cultivate a habit of finishing tasks earlier, which in turn, creates buffer periods for refinements, unexpected challenges, or even starting on the next task.

How to Execute:

1. Choose a set of tasks or projects that span over a week or a month.

2. Instead of setting deadlines based on the actual due date, set them earlier by a significant fraction, like 25% to 30%.

As you work through the tasks, monitor your completion rates concerning these early deadlines. Take note of the challenges faced, the benefits reaped, and any changes in stress levels or work quality.

Outcome: The anticipated outcome of the Early Deadline Challenge is the cultivation of a proactive mindset. When consistently practiced, this approach reduces last-minute rushes and the associated stress. Additionally, by completing tasks early, one gains a sense of accomplishment and builds momentum, leading to an overall increase in productivity. This exercise also highlights the tangible benefits of early completion, making it easier to adopt this approach in broader areas of one's professional or personal life.

CHAPTER 18

Practical Tips and Advice

Stay Adaptable

In-depth Insight: Structure in our daily schedules provides a semblance of order, making it easier to track progress and stick to our commitments. However, a common pitfall many fall into is treating this structure as sacrosanct. In a world replete with unpredictabilities, sticking to a rigid plan can often backfire. For instance, insisting on completing a task in a certain way, even when external factors have changed, can waste more time and resources than being flexible.

Adaptability is about recognizing when to pivot from the planned approach and how to do it effectively. It means understanding that while our goals remain constant, the path to achieve them might need frequent recalibrations.

Examples: Imagine a salesperson planning to meet a potential client. If the client reschedules or changes the venue last minute, rigidly sticking to the original plan or being upset about the change is counterproductive. Instead, adapting to the new scenario and using the saved time for another productive task is the hallmark of effective time management.

Daily Reflection

In-depth Insight: The idea behind daily reflection is to take a moment, at the end of the day, to assess how things went. It's about understanding what tasks were accomplished as planned, which ones veered off course, and, most importantly, why. This isn't an exercise in self-criticism but an opportunity for self-awareness and growth.

Reflection allows us to recognize patterns. Perhaps there's a specific type of task that consistently takes longer than anticipated. Or maybe external interruptions are more frequent on certain days.

Examples: Consider a project manager who notices, during her daily reflections, that team meetings always extend beyond the allocated time, causing a cascade of delays for the rest of the day. Recognizing this pattern, she can then either allocate more time for such meetings or implement strategies to make them more efficient.

Use Technology

In-depth Insight: The digital age has bestowed upon us a plethora of tools designed to enhance productivity. From task managers to digital calendars, there are apps and platforms tailored for every aspect of time management. These tools can aid in quickly rearranging tasks, setting reminders for early deadlines, or even blocking out focus periods to work without interruptions.

But technology is only as effective as its user. It's essential to not just use these tools but to use them correctly. Over-reliance without understanding can lead to more chaos than clarity.

Examples: Consider the Trello app, which uses a card-based system for task management. A content creator could set up different boards for content ideas, drafts in progress, and completed articles. If an article needs more research than anticipated, it can be easily dragged back to the "draft" board, ensuring that the workflow remains transparent and updated.

Practice Mindfulness

In-depth Insight: Mindfulness is the practice of being fully present and engaged in the current moment. In the context of time management, it means being acutely aware of what one is doing, how long it's taking, and whether it aligns with the day's goals.

By practicing mindfulness, individuals can quickly spot when they're veering off course or when an external disruption is about to throw off their schedule. It provides an opportunity to make on-the-spot adjustments, ensuring that time is used productively.

Examples: Imagine a writer working on an article. Practicing mindfulness, he notices that he's been stuck on the same paragraph for an unusually long time, perhaps indicating a need for more research or a short break. Recognizing this in the moment, rather than after an hour of unproductive struggle, allows him to adjust his approach and maintain efficiency.

CHAPTER 19

The Role of Flexibility

The Importance of Maintaining a Flexible Mindset

Flexibility is not just a principle to be applied when managing tasks and schedules; it's a state of mind. The world we navigate is dynamic, constantly evolving, and changing. As such, our plans, no matter how meticulously crafted, will often face challenges from unforeseen variables. A flexible mindset prepares us to face such challenges with poise and adaptability.

At its core, flexibility is the acknowledgment that we don't have control over everything. While this might sound daunting, it is actually liberating. By embracing uncertainty, we free ourselves from the stress and anxiety of perfection and develop resilience in the face of adversity. Flexibility also enhances creativity. When faced with an obstacle, a flexible mind searches for alternative solutions, often leading to innovative ideas and approaches that would have remained undiscovered in a rigid framework.

For instance, in today's corporate world, a flexible mindset is highly prized. Organizations deal with global challenges, changing market dynamics, technological innovations, and varying consumer behaviors. Professionals who can adapt, learn, and evolve are more likely to succeed in such an environment than those rigidly sticking to traditional methods.

Balancing Between Sticking to a Plan and Knowing When to Shift

Planning is crucial. It sets direction, establishes priorities, and serves as a roadmap to achieving our goals. However, adhering too strictly to a plan can sometimes be counterproductive. Life is filled with variables– from sudden opportunities to unexpected setbacks– and our plans need to accommodate these changes to remain effective.

The key is to strike a balance: to have a plan but not be bound by it. This means regularly evaluating and adjusting our plans based on the current reality. It's about combining the foresight of planning with the insight of the present moment.

Consider a sailor setting out to sea. While they have a planned route, they must constantly adjust their course based on the wind, currents, and other unforeseen factors. If they rigidly stick to their initial plan without accounting for these elements, they might never reach their destination, or it might take much longer than anticipated.

Real-life Examples of Where Inflexibility Led to Inefficiencies

History is replete with examples where a lack of flexibility led to significant inefficiencies or even outright failure. One classic example is the tale of Nokia. Once a dominant force in the mobile phone industry, Nokia's downfall is often attributed to its inability to adapt quickly to the rapidly changing technological landscape. While companies like Apple and Samsung embraced touchscreens and app ecosystems, Nokia clung to its traditional models for too long, leading to a loss in market share from which it never fully recovered.

In another instance, the initial response to the rise of digital photography serves as a cautionary tale. Kodak, a giant in the film photography world, initially resisted the transition to digital, believing film was superior. By the time they realized the potential of digital photography, other companies had already established dominance. Kodak's inflexibility in recognizing and adapting to industry shifts led to its decline.

These examples serve as potent reminders of the perils of inflexibility. In a world where change is the only constant, the ability to adapt and evolve isn't just a valuable trait; it's a survival skill.

CHAPTER 20

Summary: Embracing the Tactical

In our fast-paced world, where adaptability is often the key to success, the traditional approaches to time management, although foundational, may not always suffice. This chapter reiterates the essence of merging the age-old wisdom of traditional time management with the nimbleness of tactical strategies.

Blending Traditions with Tactics

The importance of traditional time management cannot be understated. Setting clear goals, planning in advance, and using tools like planners have been the bedrock of productivity for decades. However, as our tasks become more dynamic and unpredictable, there's an emerging need to adapt on-the-fly. This is where tactical time management shines. It's about being agile, anticipating the unexpected, and making real-time decisions that keep us on track. By marrying the two approaches, we harness the strengths of both, resulting in a holistic strategy that ensures consistent productivity, even when faced with unforeseen challenges.

Reflecting on Key Takeaways

Throughout the chapters, we've delved deep into various examples and exercises that illuminated the application of these concepts. One of the fundamental lessons is the value of preparedness. While we can't predict every curveball life throws at us, being prepared with tactical techniques equips us to navigate them effectively. Another vital insight is the significance of self-reflection. Regularly reviewing our actions, decisions, and outcomes helps in refining our approach, ensuring we continue to grow and improve in our time management endeavors.

The Future of Time Management

As we look ahead, it's clear that the rigid structures of the past may not always cater to the demands of the modern world. The future of time management is less about sticking rigidly to a plan and more about embracing adaptability. It's about understanding that while plans provide a roadmap, the journey might require us to take detours, shortcuts, or even entirely new routes. This doesn't signify the failure of planning but rather celebrates the human ability to adapt, innovate, and overcome.

In conclusion, as the lines between work and life continue to blur, especially in our increasingly digital age, the importance of effective time management only grows. Embracing the tactical, being agile in our approach, and continuously learning from our experiences are the keys to navigating this intricate dance of time. Whether you're a seasoned professional, a student, or anyone in between, the lessons in this chapter serve as a reminder that in the game of time, it's not just about playing the right moves but also about playing them smartly.

CHAPTER 21

Conclusion

Harmony Between Strategic and Tactical Time Management

At the heart of effective time management lies a symphony, a harmonious blend of strategy and tactics. Strategy offers us the vision, the broad strokes that provide direction, guiding us towards our goals. It's the calendar we set at the beginning of the year, the resolutions we make, and the big objectives we aim for. On the other hand, tactics represent the agile maneuvers we employ in the face of daily unpredictabilities. It's the impromptu decisions we make when a meeting runs over, the change in routine when unexpected events occur, and the split-second choices that keep our day on track. Together, these two elements intertwine to create a holistic approach to time management, ensuring that while our eyes are set on the horizon, our feet move adeptly to navigate the terrain beneath.

Embracing Change and the Unpredictable Nature of Life

Life is nothing if not unpredictable. Despite our best-laid plans and intentions, there will always be moments that catch us off guard. It's a fundamental aspect of the human experience. However, rather than perceiving this unpredictability as an adversary, we can choose to see it as an opportunity, a challenge that keeps us agile and sharpens our problem-solving skills. The true measure of our time management prowess isn't just in how well we plan, but in how effectively we adapt to change. Embracing the unpredictable ensures that we remain resilient, versatile, and ever-ready to face the myriad of surprises life has in store.

Final Thoughts on Maintaining a Balanced and Productive Life

As we conclude our journey through the realms of time management, it's essential to recognize that, at its core, effective time management is about balance. It's not just about squeezing productivity out of every second but also ensuring we have time to relax, reflect, and rejuvenate. It's about understanding that life isn't a sprint; it's a marathon. And to truly enjoy this marathon, we need moments of intensity balanced with moments of rest.

Furthermore, remember that time management isn't a destination but a journey. It requires continuous learning, adaptation, and reflection. As the landscapes of our personal and professional lives evolve, so too will our approaches to managing time. Stay curious, be open to new techniques, and most importantly, be kind to yourself.

In the grand tapestry of life, time is our most precious thread. How we choose to weave it determines the patterns, colors, and beauty of our existence. Here's to weaving a life full of purpose, passion, and memorable moments.

APPENDIX

Recommended Tools and Resources for Time Management

Digital Tools:

Trello: Trello stands out in the realm of task management tools with its intuitive, board-based design. At its core, it mimics a digital corkboard where users can create cards for individual tasks and organize them into columns or 'lists'. This visual approach makes it easy to get a snapshot of ongoing projects, prioritize tasks, and monitor progression from inception to completion. While individuals can leverage Trello for personal tasks like planning a vacation or tracking daily chores, its collaborative features, such as team boards and activity logs, also make it a favorite for project teams seeking a shared workspace.

Asana: Asana is a robust platform tailored for team collaborations. It provides a structured environment where tasks can be assigned to specific members, deadlines can be set, and dependencies can be linked. One of Asana's strengths is its ability to visualize project timelines, akin to a Gantt chart, allowing teams to track project milestones and progress seamlessly. With custom workflows and the ability to view tasks as lists, boards, or on a calendar, Asana offers a flexible space that can be adapted to various project management styles.

RescueTime: In the digital age, where distractions are just a click away, understanding how we spend our time online has become paramount. RescueTime addresses this need by running discreetly in the background of devices, tracking application and website usage. With its insightful reports, users can identify productivity sinks, set goals, and even block distracting sites. By shining a light on digital habits, RescueTime equips individuals with the knowledge they need to make informed decisions about their online behaviors and boost productivity.

Todoist: Todoist is a comprehensive to-do list application that goes beyond simple task tracking. Its clean interface allows users to quickly jot down tasks, set priorities, and assign due dates. What sets Todoist apart is its adaptability– it can handle anything from one-off reminders to complex projects with multiple participants.

Its recurring task feature ensures that routine tasks don't fall by the wayside, and integrations with various platforms mean that it can fit seamlessly into numerous workflows.

Focus@Will: In a unique blend of science and art, Focus@Will utilizes the power of music to enhance concentration. Drawing from neuroscience research, it offers a curated selection of tracks designed to engage the brain's limbic system, thus fostering a state of flow. Unlike regular music streaming platforms, Focus@Will's tracks are purposefully crafted to minimize distractions, making it an ideal companion for those looking to drown out external noise and tune into their tasks.

Resources:

Time Management Seminars: In a world where time is often considered the most valuable asset, mastering its management is crucial for personal and professional success. Time Management Seminars, such as those offered by reputable institutions like the American Management Association or Dale Carnegie Training, play an instrumental role in this regard. These workshops provide participants with practical skills and insights to enhance their productivity, prioritize tasks effectively, and strike a balance between work and leisure. Typically, these seminars combine theoretical knowledge with hands-on activities, ensuring attendees can apply learned concepts in real-world scenarios. With experts at the helm and the backing of renowned institutions, these seminars offer a holistic approach to mastering the art and science of time management.

Pomodoro Technique Timer: The Pomodoro Technique, founded by Francesco Cirillo, has taken the productivity world by storm with its simplicity and effectiveness. The principle is to work intensely for 25 minutes, termed a "Pomodoro", followed by a short break, with the cycle repeating. To aid in this technique, several digital Pomodoro Technique Timers have been developed. These timers, available as web applications, desktop software, or mobile apps, assist users in sticking to the Pomodoro intervals. They come equipped with features like sound alerts, long break intervals after a set number of Pomodoros, and tracking capabilities to monitor productivity. By providing a structured approach to work and rest, these timers make implementing the Pomodoro Technique seamless and more impactful.

Further Reading Suggestions

"Getting Things Done" by David Allen: In the realm of productivity literature, David Allen's "Getting Things Done" stands as a beacon. More than just a guide, it introduces a holistic methodology to manage tasks, ensuring that nothing falls through the cracks. Allen emphasizes the importance of having a clear mind and a system to capture all tasks, freeing the brain from the stress of remembering. The book offers actionable strategies, from organizing tasks to setting priorities, ensuring that you can navigate through life's complexities with clarity and efficiency.

"Deep Work" by Cal Newport: At a time when distractions are the norm, Cal Newport's "Deep Work" serves as an essential guide for those seeking to achieve profound, valuable work. Newport argues that in our digital age, the ability to focus without distraction on a demanding task is becoming increasingly rare and thus, increasingly valuable. The book sheds light on the benefits of deep, focused work and provides methodologies to cultivate this skill, distinguishing oneself in the professional field and achieving cognitive breakthroughs.

"The 4-Hour Work Week" by Timothy Ferriss: Timothy Ferriss challenges the conventional 9-5 work life in his groundbreaking book "The 4-Hour Work Week." He introduces readers to the idea of living more and working less through automation, outsourcing, and escaping the typical work constraints. With engaging anecdotes and actionable advice, Ferriss navigates concepts of time freedom, financial independence, and a redefined view of retirement, encouraging readers to create their own luxury lifestyle design.

"The 7 Habits of Highly Effective People" by Stephen R. Covey: Stephen R. Covey's masterpiece, "The 7 Habits of Highly Effective People," has influenced countless readers worldwide. Going beyond mere productivity tips, Covey presents a principle-centered approach for both personal and interpersonal effectiveness. From "Being Proactive" to "Sharpening the Saw," the seven habits provide a timeless and holistic approach to life and work, pushing readers to think deeply about their values, goals, and relationships.

"Essentialism: The Disciplined Pursuit of Less" by Greg McKeown: In a world that constantly demands more, Greg McKeown's "Essentialism" is a breath of fresh air, reminding readers of the value of less but better. McKeown delves into the concept of "essentialism", urging individuals to discern the vital few from the trivial many. By focusing on what's truly essential, one can lead a more purposeful and productive life. The book offers insights into making better choices about where to spend one's time and energy, ensuring that they align with one's truest intentions and goals.

ABOUT THE AUTHOR

Prakash Rao wears many hats with grace, effortlessly weaving between the diverse worlds of engineering, music, literature, and education. Each chapter of his life story speaks to his tenacity, passion, and unparalleled dedication to his crafts.

An engineer by training, Prakash's journey through time management was born not out of necessity but of ambition. With an insatiable appetite for knowledge and a desire to pursue a myriad of interests, he transformed the challenges of time into opportunities.

With over a dozen books across various genres, he has not only proved his literary prowess but has also showcased his commitment to sharing knowledge, perspectives, and life lessons with readers across the world.

While literature might capture his words, music captures his soul. An esteemed performer of the South Indian classical (Carnatic) drum, the mridangam, he boasts of an illustrious musical journey spanning over 44 years. With almost 3000 concerts under his belt, his beats and rhythms echo his deep-rooted connection to this art form.

But Prakash's story doesn't stop at books and beats. He has navigated a successful career in the realm of software, scaling heights from a developer to a director, and branching out as an independent consultant. His experiences as an Adjunct Professor at two esteemed colleges and his current role in training young minds to optimize their learning skills further underline his versatility and commitment to education.

"Tactical Time Management" is more than just another book; it's a life-changing process. Where many time management gurus speak of planning (strategy), Prakash speaks of actions (tactics). We don't get results from plans although planning is an essential part of getting results – we get results only from taking action. And not any action – effective and efficient action.

Dive into these pages to experience a world where good tactics lead to better time management. With Prakash Rao as your guide, you're in for an enlightening journey.